We Shall Be Free!

We Shall Be Free!

*Black Communist Protests
in Seven Voices*

Walter T. Howard

TEMPLE UNIVERSITY PRESS
Philadelphia

WALTER T. HOWARD is Professor of American History at Bloomsburg University in northeastern Pennsylvania. He is the editor of *B. D. Amis, African American Radical: A Short Anthology of His Writings and Speeches* and the author of *Lynchings: Extralegal Violence in Florida during the 1930s* as well as *Black Communists Speak on Scottsboro: A Documentary History* (Temple).

TEMPLE UNIVERSITY PRESS
Philadelphia, Pennsylvania 19122
www.temple.edu/tempress

Library of Congress Cataloging-in-Publication Data

Howard, Walter T., 1951–
    We shall be free! : black communist protests in seven voices /
Walter T. Howard.
        pages   cm
    Includes bibliographical references and index.
    ISBN 978-1-4399-0859-4 (cloth : alk. paper)
    ISBN 978-1-4399-0861-7 (e-book)
    1. African American communists. 2. African Americans—Civil rights—
History—20th century. 3. Civil rights and socialism—United States—
History—20th century. 4. Communism—United States—History—20th
century. I. Title.

    HX86.H793 2013
    324.273'75092396073—dc23   2012040898

Printed in the United States of America

2 4 6 8 9 7 5 3 1

Dedicated to my family:
Virginia, Ian, Austin, Chris,
Nicholas, and Stephanie

Contents

Preface and Acknowledgments

We Shall Be Free! seeks to break new ground in the scholarship of the African American Left. More specifically, it addresses a particular historical need to give voice to black Communists and to respect the intellectual contributions found in their protest writings. To be sure, a number of the "new historians" of American Communism have written about the history of the Communist Party of the United States of America (CPUSA) and race; however, few have provided an adequate forum for black Communists to speak for themselves over a wide range of vital issues. By focusing on seven historical figures, and the documents and essays they wrote, this book attempts to give voice to an important section of the African American community whose thought has been minimized, discounted, or overlooked altogether by the historical profession in general.

The seven black Communists examined in this tome were chosen for their historical significance based on a long-term productive commitment to the party and "the cause." I have omitted celebrity Communists such as Paul Robeson, who never joined the CPUSA, and relative short-timers such as Richard Wright, who eventually left the party. Also, I have not included more recent black Communists such as Angela Davis and Amiri Baraka. These two heavyweight notables, who are still contributing to American radical history, deserve entire monographs. And no doubt, some graduate students and professional historians are currently working on projects that deal with their careers. Finally, there is in the epilogue an entry by W.E.B. Du Bois, who resisted joining the CPUSA until the end of his long life. The chosen seven black Communists—B. D. Amis, Harry Haywood, James W. Ford, Benjamin J. Davis Jr., Louise Thompson Patterson, William L. Patterson, and Claudia Jones—represent a diverse group in terms of their ideas, gender, backgrounds, and personalities. Nonetheless, there is unity in diversity. The unifying theme in their protest thought is the effort to foster a black "culture of resistance" to white racism and to the disvalues inherent in capitalism as an economic, social, and cultural system. Furthermore, in terms of a time frame, this book reveals the breadth and depth of the political and social dissent of key African American Communists from the Jazz Age through the Great Depression to the modern Civil Right Movement. What is more, the acute need for such a study lies in the present-day political situation in the early twenty-first century.

Today we have the nation's first African American president addressing major issues of worldwide economic recession, numerous wars, and even genocide. Although President Barack Obama's pragmatic policies in response to these problems fall within the mainstream of Western capitalism and political democracy, the hysterical American Right screams that the president is a foreign-born Communist or Socialist. Needless to say, no rational person could accept as true these paranoid fantasies. In light of these nonsensical allegations, it might be instructive to look at the well-documented historical record from the middle of the twentieth century, when reality-based tribulations such as depression, war, and genocide were actually addressed by genuine black Communists.

Indeed, black Communists, from the 1920s to the early 1960s, were authentic American radicals who offered multifaceted ideas and analyses during an era of great change in U.S. and world history. Subsequently, because of race, gender, and ideology, most mainstream historians have ignored or distorted the voice of this segment of the African American community. From the Great Depression to World War II and the early years of the Cold War, black Communists fought fearlessly on the front lines in the black freedom struggle within the United States at the same time that they condemned white colonialism, global racism, and genocide. Few historians have focused in any meaningful way on what African American Communists—who were committed activists for social justice—had to say about these vital historical matters.

This survey of the responses of African American Communists to the Great Depression, World War II, and the Cold War draws on many fresh sources from FBI files, as well as documents from Moscow. The holdings of the Russian State Archives of Social and Political History (formerly the Russian Center for the Preservation and Study of Documents of Contemporary History) are separated into a number of "fonds," or collections. Research for this book concentrated primarily on one deposit, Fond 515, documents of the CPUSA. I have also used documents from the Tamiment Library and Robert F. Wagner Labor Archives at New York University, the Louise Thompson Patterson Papers at Emory University, and the Earl Browder Papers at Syracuse University. Finally, Carole Boyce Davies, biographer of Claudia Jones, was kind enough to share important material with me.

Prologue

The CPUSA and Black America, 1919–1928

For the duration of the "Red Summer" of 1919, in the midst of the disorder that followed World War I and in the exhilaration stimulated by the Russian Revolution, white radicals in the United States kicked off the American Communist movement. Its birth was accompanied by an eruption of major race riots in this country that signaled a new militant resistance by young blacks to American racial proscription. "New Negro" intellectuals gave voice to this militancy. Some of them, expressing solidarity with the pro-Bolshevik uprisings occurring in Europe at the time, were struck by Bolshevism's appeal not only to the working class of highly industrialized nations but also to oppressed national ethnic minorities.

In spite of this interest, however, few blacks enlisted in the new radical movement. In the early years of the history of the CPUSA in the United States, this new Marxist-Leninist organization claimed few African American members. Most party devotees came from foreign-language federations formerly associated with the Socialist Party of America (SP). Moreover, these immigrant workers from Eastern and Southern Europe did not have much positive contact with black Americans. The source of the negligence can indeed be traced to the Socialist Party.

The SP had attracted few African American members in the years before 1919. True, Eugene Debs and other prominent Socialist leaders *were usually opponents of racial segregation, disenfranchisement, peonage, and lynching. Nevertheless, American Socialists did not emphasize work with blacks, and they often downplayed or ignored white supremacy in the form of their party's allegiance to trade unions that discriminated against non-white workers. Historians generally agree that the SP was unwilling to combat vigorously the racial inequities among American workers.*

Communists in the United States, like the Socialists, at first displayed only a slight concern with black workers. They also failed to engage the young black militants who emerged on the scene in the postwar period. By the early 1920s, however, the CPUSA was defining the "Negro problem" in the United States in a global context. As an instrument of world revolution and anticolonialism, the CPUSA approached the racial situation from that broad perspective. Accordingly, black Americans combating Jim Crow and lynching were essentially no different from Africans fighting for national independence and self-determination. Not surprisingly, then, the party proved most attractive at this time to black laborers who displayed internationalist proclivities. In fact, a number of African American members of the CPUSA in the early 1920s were immigrant workers from the West Indies. Understandably, they viewed the struggles of the black working class in the United States in the larger context of non-Europeans fighting against capitalism and imperialism. ▪

During the middle of the 1920s, some leaders of the African Blood Brotherhood (ABB), a black Socialist organization that boasted a number of black Jamaican radicals in its ranks, linked up with the CPUSA. A black Marxist organization active during the Harlem Renaissance, the ABB also opposed American participation in World War I and linked the struggle for black liberation in the United States to the battle against European colonization in Africa. In 1918, Briggs started a new magazine called The Crusade. *The ABB backed the electoral campaigns of the SP candidate A. Philip Randolph and exposed lynching in the South and job discrimination in the North. Briggs believed that the African American's true place was with the labor and that blacks would benefit from the triumph of labor and the destruction of the "Capital Civilization." A secret revolutionary organization, the ABB's purpose and program was the liberation of African people and the redemption of the African race. Its program emphasized racial pride, Black National-*

ism, Pan-Africanism, and an economic analysis of the African American struggle that linked it to colonialism and imperialism. By 1925, the ABB leadership had established close ties with the CPUSA.

The following FBI document, which focuses on the ABB and the historical black figure Claude McKay (the FBI worried he was too close to the Communists because of his visits to the Soviet Union), reveals important historical information but no real subversion. Claude McKay (1889–1948), a Jamaican American writer and poet, was an influential figure in the Harlem Renaissance. He was also attracted to communism in his early life; however, he was never a member of the American Communist Party.

■ ■ ■

Federal Bureau of Investigation, Freedom of Information Privacy Act, File on Claude McKay

Excerpt from the 1922 Report on the Commission of the Fourth Conference of the Communist International

Individuals
Claude McKay

Negro radical and one of the editors of the "Liberator," is said to have made the statement recently that this publication may have to suspend publication because of lack of funds, brought about by the embezzlement of $4000, by one of the employees. McKay, at the same time stated that he is still a member of the Communist Party and intends to rejoin the I.W.W.

While at Ray Baker's office, 7 E. 15th Street, Room 401, McKay stated that he supported a true militant class conscious movement, which is not afraid to use guns, and that in the Tulsa riots last year the African Blood Brotherhood supplied the Negroes with the guns and load in the fighting there, which might also be said of other race riots.

He was asked where he secured his information, and stated he has firsthand information of this, but refused to divulge the name.

Baker is a close friend of Claude McKay, and it is believed this is the source of information.

Some months ago while placing Cyril Briggs [another black Communist] under surveillance in connection with the African Blood Brotherhood, mention [redacted] to a house West 133rd Street, with a man who was described at that time, and that Claude McKay was also [redacted] believed that that man is one A. J. Anderson. . . .

▪ ▪ ▪

In his classic Hammer and Hoe: Alabama Communists during the Great Depression, *Robin D. G. Kelley successfully established that the Communist movement raised black consciousness by placing the Southern racial caste system (the system of segregation, disenfranchisement, and lynching) in a global context. The following essay by the black Communist Otto Huiswoud reinforces this historical point.*

▪ ▪ ▪

Earl Browder Papers, Special Collections Research Center, Syracuse University Library

World Aspects of the Negro Question

By Otto Huiswoud★

The Communist, 1930

★Otto Huiswoud was born in 1893 in Suriname, the grandson of a slave. In 1912 he moved to the United States where he worked as a trader in tropical products and, later, as a printer in Harlem. He then became involved with American socialist and Negro organizations. His earliest known affiliation was with a group surrounding the *Messenger,* a monthly magazine established by A. Philip Randolph (1889–1979) and Chandler Owen (1889–1967) and published from 1917 to 1928. While urging American Negroes to support the Russian Revolution, this group's leaders rejected the Communists' greater emphasis on class struggle, rather than on racism. . . .

UNTIL RECENT YEARS the Negro question and its relationship to the revolutionary working class movement was practically unnoticed, almost completely ignored. Little attention was paid to the

Negro masses in their struggles against imperialist exploitation and subjection, no thought given to their revolutionary potentialities—to the role they are destined to play in the movement for the emancipation of the working class from capitalist domination and enslavement. As a result, little or no attempts were made to draw the Negro workers in the struggle against world imperialism.

Our approach to the Negro question has not only been largely sectional rather than international, but our concept and interpretation of the Negro question was narrow and incorrect. The old Social Democratic notion that the Negro question is only a class question, prevailed with us for a considerable time. We are only now beginning to realize that the Negro question is not only a class question but also a race question. (We are beginning to understand that the Negro masses are not only subjected to the ordinary forms of exploitation as other workers, but that they are also the victims of a brutal caste system which holds them as an inferior servile class; that lynching, segregation, peonage, etc., are some of the means utilized to keep them the underdog in capital society—social outcasts.)

In order to maintain its policy of repression, violence and exploitation of the Negro, the bourgeoisie creates a false racial ideology among the whites and fosters contempt and hatred for the Negros. The idea of "superior" and "inferior" races is the theoretical justifications for their policy of super-exploitation of the Negro race.

The situation of the Negro masses varies in the different countries and therefore requires investigation and analysis. The concrete application of the policies and tasks of the Communist Parties are dependent upon the prevailing conditions in the various countries. It is the utmost importance that we note the differences that characterize the position If the Negroes in the different parts of the world. The following territorial division based upon population and certain general common features should be considered:

The United States and some Latin American countries, in which the Negro population is a minority.

Africa and the West Indies, where the Negro population is the majority is relation to the white population.

The "independent" Negro nations (Haiti and Liberia), which are in reality semi-colonies of American imperialism.

While the Negro race everywhere is a subject race and there exists a common bond of interest based upon racial oppression, nevertheless, the conditions of the Negroes are not similar in the above mentioned territorial divisions. It is essential that we distinguish the situation of the Negro masses in the colonies—Africa and the West Indies; the semi-colonies—Haiti and Liberia, who suffer from colonial exploitation, from that of the Negro in America, a racial minority, subjected to racial persecution and exploitation. We must take into consideration the National-colonial character of the Negro question in Africa and the West Indies and the racial character of this question in the United States.

We must take note of the fact that the Negro question in Africa has all the characteristic features of the national-colonial question. Some of these features are:

> *Majority of population and organized communities.*
> *A common language and culture. In contrast to this Negro in America has:*
> *No distinct language and culture from the dominant racial group; it is a minority of the population; its only distinguishing feature is its racial origin.*

It is therefore imperative that the concrete policies and tasks of the Communist Parties be based on the foregoing considerations. Only with a clear understanding of these conditions can we apply the correct policies and tactics. . . .

The Negro in the United States

In the United States the Negro is an oppressed racial minority. The exploitation of the Negro masses in America is of a twofold character—racial and class exploitation. The twelve million Negroes in the United States are the special victims of capitalist exploitation and subjection. Members of a racial minority, they are singled out for the severest attacks and persecution by the employing class.

The development of America required cheap labor for the southern cotton and tobacco plantations. Africa became the source of supply of the much needed man-power. The slave trade, while resulting in the death of millions of Africans, the depopulations on a wholesale scale of the African Continent, and in the most horrible violence and atrocities against the African natives, produced millions in profits for the slave traders and their bankers.

Chained to the land for over 300 years through the system of chattel slavery, Negro labor produced the basis of the wealth of the United States. Driven with the lash, subjected to the most horrible forms of torture and brutality, the Negro slaves produced untold riches for the ruling class. The many revolts of the slaves against this monstrous system of enslavement and exploitation were brutally suppressed by the wealthy landowners and the State. Following the Civil War, the primitive mode of production of chattel slavery was replaced with that of wage slavery.

However, while the Negroes in the North became wage slaves during the period of reconstruction, the Southern Negro was practically completely re-enslaved on the plantations. The courts enacted innumerable laws which served to keep the Negro under the complete domination of the landowners. Every instrument at its disposal was used by the ruling class to shackle the Negro workers and bind them to the plantation.

The South

The Negro population is not only concentrated in the South, but the bulk is concentrated in the rural sections. Out of the nearly 9,000,000 Negroes living in sixteen Southern states, about 6,000,000 or two-thirds live in the rural areas. In a number of states the Negro masses form a large part of the population. In Alabama and Louisiana, they constitute (1920 census) 38%, in Georgia 42% and in Mississippi and South Carolina 51% of the total population.

In the South the millions of Negro workers and farmers are largely concentrated within certain areas known as the "Black Belt," due primarily to the plantation type of agriculture. The Negro tenant farmer, share cropper, and farm worker are virtually slaves on the land. The poor farmer and share cropper can never hope to own the land he tills, due to a credit and mortgage system which chains him to the land and makes him the serf of the merchants, landholders and bankers. Not only the land, but even the implements, crops—everything is mortgages, placing them under complete domination of the white ruling class. The Negro farm workers are compelled to toil long hours under the most revolting conditions and for a miserable pittance as wages, receiving in some instances, as in Georgia, as little as $19 per month. Peonage, debt and convict slavery, vagrancy laws, disfranchisements, segregation, lynching and mob violence are the methods used to mercilessly exploit and oppress the Negroes in the South. These are the methods of double exploitation of the Negro used by the capitalist class in order to extract super profits from their labor.

The migratory movement of the Negroes from the Southern plantations which really began soon after the Civil War and reached its peak in 1923, resulted in the tremendous increase of the Negro population in the Southern as well as the Northern cities. Fully one and one-half million Negroes have migrated to the urban centers between the years of 1910 and 1920. In 1890 less than 1,500,000 Negroes lived in cities. Recent estimates give the urban Negro population as 4,000,000. Between the years of 1920 [and 19]25 the Negro farm population decreased from 5,300,615 to 4,505,796 or 15%. During this same period the white farm population decreased 11% indicating that Negroes were migrating from the farms at a greater ratio than whites.[1] The latest reports give the total number of Negro farmers as 926,708. Of this number 219,612 are farm owners, 2,026 farm managers, and 705,708 tenants. Negro farmers are 14.7% of the total number of farmers. In 1910, 27% of Negro male laborers were farm workers, in 1920 only 16.5%.

The rapid industrialization of the south is drawing ever larger numbers of Negroes into the southern industries. The process of rationalization, speed-up, etc., affects most sharply the Negro workers. Fresh from farm labor, they come into industry for the first time at a point where the most terrific drive for production is taking place. Driven at a terrific rate, at long hours, and miserably low wages, terrorized and victimized, Negro labor in the South is not only cheap labor, but virtually slave labor. The south depends to a very large extent upon Negro labor for the production of its wealth. The heaviest, dirtiest tasks are performed by Negro workers. The turpentine, lumber, fertilizer, tobacco and cotton industries use largely Negro labor. Over 50% of the more than 100,000 lumber workers in the South are Negroes. Nearly three times as many Negroes are whites

---

[1] These figures are national, but the Negro farmers are mostly in the South.

are in the steel industry working ten hours and more per pay. Over 50,000 are in the coal mining industry. The tobacco and cotton industries employ tens of thousands of Negro workers, paying them as low as ten dollars per week. The vast majority of waterfront workers in the South are Negroes. The textile industry is increasing using Negro workers. One textile plant in Durham, N.C. employs 700 Negro workers.

Negro women and children are used to further worsen the conditions of the male workers. Negro women and children are employed largely in the tobacco and textile industries, slaughtering and meat packing houses and the canneries. Twenty-nine and one-half percent of Negro women in canneries earn less than four dollars per week. The average wage for tobacco workers is seven dollars per week. In the cotton waste mills 81% of the Negro women employed toil ten hours per day for a miserably low wage.

Segregation into the worst sections, compelled to live in flimsy, dirty shanties, jim-crowed at every turn, the Negro masses are bitterly exploited and live in the most abject poverty. They are disfranchised and subjected to violence if they dare assert their rights to vote in elections. Intimidated and brutally lynched by the Ku Klux Klan, the Night Riders and various other terroristic agencies of the capitalist class, the Negro masses in the South are unable to resist their oppression and exploitation, because of the lack of organization and the prejudiced attitude, not only of the employers, but also of the white workers who are saturated with the idea of race "superiority." Blinded by race hatred, deliberately fostered by the capitalist class, the mass of white workers fail to see the common interest between them and the Negro workers. (Despite this racial antagonism, the worsening of the conditions of the white workers practically to the level of that the Negroes, and the organizing and propaganda activities of the left wing unions and the Communist Party are laying the basis for the united action on the part of black and white against their common enemy—the exploiters.)

The North

Soon after the Civil War, a slow but steady migration of Negroes from the South to the North began. Thousands of Negro peasants abandoned the plantations for the Northern cities. The demand for labor in the war industries and the check on foreign immigration provided the basis for a huge mass movement from the South to the North, involving hundreds of thousands of Negroes. The Negro population of the North increased tremendously. The following table will show a partial picture of the increase of the Negro population in some of the industrial states:

States	1870	1920
Pennsylvania	65,294	284,568
Ohio	63,213	186,187
New York	52,081	198,483
New Jersey	30,658	117,132
Illinois	28,762	182,274
Indiana	24,560	80,810

Turning their backs to the oppressive conditions of the South, with its intense exploitation, low wages and long hours, peonage and terrorism, the migrants flocked into the North. In his efforts to escape the open terrorism, Jim-Crowism and serfdom in the South, the Negro soon discovered that the conditions in the North are only little better than those from which he escaped. In the North he is the special object of intense exploitation and proscription. He is confronted with discrimination and Jim-Crowism in restaurants, theatres and other public places. He is the special prey of the landlords and real estate sharks. The segregation of Negroes into restricted areas, forcing them to pay rents forty to fifty percent higher than white tenants pay for similar accommodations, is one of the methods of double exploitation utilized by the bourgeoisie against the Negro. Both white and Negro landlords reap a harvest of profits through this system of segregating Negroes into districts notorious for their unsanitary conditions, thereby causing a shockingly high death rate of the Negro workers. Racial separation, through segregation, is an effective means of reducing the Negro to a social outcast.

The Negro farmhand of yesterday has become an industrial worker in the North. Absorbed into various industries, the two million Negro workers are an important factor in the basic industries, such as steel, coal, iron, automobile, railroad, etc.

The industrialization of the Negro workers can best be appreciated when we take into consideration not only the increase of Negro

population in the industrial areas of the country but also the large
numbers who have entered into some of the basic industries. The
role and importance of the Negro proletariat in the North can easily be seen from the following figures, though incomplete:

Occupation	1890	1910	1920
Trade & transportation	145,717	334,442	452,888
Extraction of minerals	—	—	73,229
Mfg. & mechanical	207,588	522,581	886,810
Textile	—	11,333	24,734
TOTAL	353,305	898,336	1,437,661

Taking his place side by side with the white workers in the
gigantic factories, mills and mines, subjected to capitalist rationalization, wage cuts, speed-up and unemployment, with its conse-
quent radicalization of the masses, the role of the Negro proletariat
will play in the sharpening class struggles can no longer be ignored.
The Negro workers are largely unorganized as a result of the
A.F. of L. policy of outright refusal to organize the mass of semi-
skilled and unskilled workers. The reactionary bureaucracy in control of the craft unions bar Negroes outright or practice gross discrimination against them. With their policy of racial separation and
hostility, they play the game of the employers. The A.F. of L. and
socialist leaders constantly betray the Negro workers in their struggle, as in the waiters' strike in Chicago in 1922, the calling off of the
scheduled Pullman porters' strike and the issuing of a "Federal
Charter" to the Brotherhood of Sleeping Car Porters, thereby jim-
crowing and weakening the organization, leaving the workers at the
mercy of the Pullman Company. In spite of the treacherous policy
of these labor "leaders" there are nearly 200,000 Negro workers
organized in the trade unions.

The sharpening class differentiation within the Negro population must no longer be ignored. The segregation of the Negro
masses creates the basis for the development of a group of real
estate brokers, merchants and bankers. Under the deceptive slogan
of "race loyalty" the Negro bourgeoisie has been able to establish
an ideological influence over the Negro masses.

The Garvey movement and the N.A.A.C.P. are classic examples of the reformist movements exerting considerable ideological

influence over the Negro, diverting his militancy into reformist channels, betraying the Negro workers in their struggle against capitalist
exploitation.

A basic task before the Communist Party and the revolutionary
unions is the winning over of the Negro masses in America and in
the colonies for their struggle against world imperialism, under the
leadership of the Communist International.

The recent revolts of the natives throughout Africa are indica-
tive of the readiness of the African workers to fight against the brutal exploitation and oppression of world imperialism. The colonial
slaves in Africa and the West Indies must be organized and drawn
into the world-wide revolutionary movement for the overthrow of
world capitalism.

In the United States the proletarianization and the growing radicalization of the Negro masses provide us the basis for organizing
the Negro industrial workers in the new revolutionary trade unions
under the leadership of the Trade Union Unity League. The atten-
dance and active participation of sixty-four Negro delegates at the
Cleveland Convention of the T.U.U.L is a sign of the awakening of
the Negro workers and their readiness for joint struggle with the
white workers against capitalist rationalization and enslavement.

The Communist Party must throw all its energy; mobilize all
its forces for the winning of the millions of Negro workers and
farmers for the revolution. The peculiar forms of racial exploitation
of the Negro masses provide the basis for a race liberation movement which must be actively supported by the Communist Party.
Our slogan of race equality as well as political and social equality
must be translated into action and the Party must become the
champion and the active organizer of the oppressed Negro race for
full emancipation. Gastonia proves to us the possibilities of smash-
ing the age-old Southern traditions and prejudices, mobilizing the
white and black workers for common struggle against exploitation
and oppression.

The danger of another imperialist war and of a war against the
Soviet Union, into which thousands of Negroes will be drawn and
sacrificed to appease the greed of world imperialism in their scheme
for the re-division of the world, must be utilized to mobilize the
Negro workers for struggle against world capitalism.

It is the duty of our Party to mobilize and rally the masses of white workers in defense to the Negro workers, linking up the struggles of the white with that of the black workers through all of its campaigns and activities.

A determined fight must be waged against every manifestation of white chauvinism among the broad masses of white workers and a campaign to stamp out all neglect and indifference among our white comrades toward Negro work

The Party must intensify its work among the Negro masses, drawing them into the Party, aiding in the strengthening and building up of the American Negro Labor Congress and mobilizing the Negro Workers under our leadership.

Chronology

The CPUSA and African Americans

1917	Bolsheviks, led by Lenin, seize power in Russia.
1919	Communist Party of America (CP) and Communist Labor Party (CLP) founded in the United States. Both parties go underground in imitation of the Bolsheviks and in reply to U.S. government harassment.
1921	Under pressure from the Communist International (Comintern), the two American parties merged and form the Workers Party (WP), later renamed the Communist Party of the United States of America (CPUSA).
1919–1923	The newly founded Communist movement has almost no African American adherents. Most of its members, from various foreign-language federations of the Socialist Party of America, consists of workers who often have little or no interaction with black Americans.
1919–1925	*African Blood Brotherhood (ABB).* The ABB, a radical black liberation group founded in 1919 in New York City by the journalist Cyril Briggs, is established as a propaganda organization built on the model of the secret society.

1920s   *West Indian Communists.* During its early years,
the CP has the greatest appeal to black workers
who are internationalist in their orientation. Subsequently, in the 1920s it begins to recruit African
Americans as members. The most prominent black
CP members at this time are largely immigrants
from the West Indies who regard the black worker's
struggle as part of the wider crusades against capitalism and imperialism.

1922   *Fourth Congress of the Comintern.* The poet
Claude McKay (Jamaica) and Otto Huiswoud
(Suriname) convince the Comintern to set up a
transnational Negro Commission that seeks to unite
all movements of black people battling colonialism.

1925   *The American Negro Labor Congress (ANLC).*
The Comintern guides the CP in 1924 to renew its
efforts to organize African Americans. In response,
the CP forms the ANLC in 1925. The ANLC
attacks the NAACP and other similar organizations
as middle-class accommodationists controlled by
white patrons.

1920s   *Universal Negro Improvement Association
(UNIA).* During the 1920s, the ANLC and the
CP view Marcus Garvey's UNIA as ideologically
unsound. Although the CP supports Garvey's
notion of "race consciousness," it sharply contests
his support for a separate black nation and his support of black capitalism. When the party attempts
to enlist followers of the UNIA, Garvey expels the
CP members and sympathizers in its ranks.

1928–1935   *National Self-Determination.* The Sixth Congress
of the Comintern (1928) changes the CPUSA's
racial policy. The party now asserts that African
Americans in the Southern states make up a separate national group and that black sharecroppers
and tenant farmers in the South constitute an incip-

ient revolutionary force. Consequently, the Comintern instructs the party to press the demand for a separate nation for blacks within the so-called Black Belt, a swath of counties with a majority-black population extending from eastern Virginia and the Carolinas through central Georgia, Alabama, the delta regions of Mississippi and Louisiana, and the coastal areas of Texas.

1930s *CPUSA in the Deep South.* The CPUSA sends organizers to the Deep South for the first time in the late 1920s. The party focuses its energy, for the most part, on specific issues, such as the organization of miners, steelworkers, and tenant farmers; utility shutoffs; evictions; jobs; unemployment benefits; lynching; and the pervasive system of Jim Crow.

1925–1946 *The International Labor Defense (ILD).* The ILD, as the established legal defense organization for the Communist movement beginning in 1925, replaces the Labor Defense Council (the party's previous legal defense organization). Led by William L. Patterson, the ILD might best be described as the U.S. section of the International Red Aid organization. During its history, the ILD defends Sacco and Vanzetti, actively supports the civil rights and anti-lynching movements, and participates in the defense of the Scottsboro youths. In 1946, the ILD merges with the National Federation for Constitutional Liberties to form the Civil Rights Congress (CRC).

1930s–1940s *The Scottsboro Case.* The CPUSA's most productive work in the South is undoubtedly its defense, through the ILD, of the "Scottsboro Nine." These young black men, detained in 1931 following a scrap with white youths, are wrongly convicted and sentenced to death after falsely being charged with raping two white women later found on the same train.

1930s   *Angelo Herndon.* The Scottsboro defense is not
the only concern of the ILD's many cases in the
South at that time. The ILD also defends Angelo
Herndon, a CPUSA activist sentenced to death by
the State of Georgia for treason for his advocacy of
national self-determination for blacks in the Black
Belt while demanding retribution for lynching and
due process for criminal defendants. For a time in
the early and mid-1930s, the ILD is the most active
defender of blacks' civil rights in the South and the
most popular party organization among African
Americans.

1930–1935   *The League of Struggle for Negro Rights (LSNR).*
The LSNR, created in 1930 as the successor to the
ANLC, is especially effective in coordinating assistance for the Scottsboro defendants. It also crusades
for a separate black nation in the South and against
police brutality and Jim Crow laws.

1935–1947   *National Negro Congress (NNC).* The broadly
based NNC isthe successor to the LSNR. It represents the apex of the CPUSA's Depression-era
struggle to bond black and white workers, as well as
American intellectuals, in the fight for racial justice.
The NNC opposes war, fascism, and discrimination—especially racial discrimination. The NNC
disbands in 1947 because of Cold War suppression.

1935–1939   *The Popular Front.* In 1935, the Comintern aban-
dons Third Period ultra-leftism in favor of a Popu-
lar Front strategy. This new policy wants to unite
socialist and liberal non-socialist organizations
around the shared focus of anti-fascism. Consequently, the CPUSA repairs its relations with middle-
class groups such as the NAACP and even fosters
associations with church groups, principally in the
North. The CPUSA also begins to support the
New Deal by curbing its criticisms of the Roosevelt
administration.

1930s–1940s *Communists and African American Culture.* During the Popular Front years, the CPUSA attracts support from some of the most important figures in African American literature, such as Ralph Ellison, Chester Himes, Langston Hughes, and Richard Wright. Some of these black writers even join the party. However, some break with it in later years. A vocal defender of the Soviet Union, Paul Robeson stands out as an enthusiastic supporter of the Soviet system.

1940 *The Smith Act.* The Smith Act makes it a crime to advocate the overthrow of the U.S. government. Although it is aimed at Nazis in the United States during World War II, the law is later used against American Communists to outlaw the CPUSA.

1939–1941 *The Nazi–Soviet Pact.* The signing of the Molotov–Ribbentrop Pact damages the CPUSA significantly in the black community. The black Socialist A. Philip Randolph resigns from the NNC in protest, and black newspapers throughout the North condemn the party for its reverse in opposition to Nazism.

1941–1945 *World War II after the Nazi–Soviet Pact.* When Adolf Hitler's forces invade the Soviet Union in June 1941, the CPUSA reverses its position once again, this time to all-out support for the war effort against Hitler. It denounces Randolph's proposed March on Washington against employment discrimination in war industries, arguing that the action might harm production. But the CPUSA still demands that defense contractors integrate and takes steps to combat "hate strikes" and white-led race riots in Detroit.

1950 *McCarran-Walter Internal Security Act.* Congress passes the McCarran-Walter Internal Security Act to monitor Communists in the United States.

1946–1956   *Civil Rights Congress (CRC).* Founded in Detroit in 1946, the CRC emerges out of the union of three groups with links to the CPUSA: the ILD, the NNC, and the National Federation for Constitutional Liberties. Exemplifying the attitude and methods of all three of its precursors, the CRC focuses on legal defense and mass political action on behalf of class victims of the Cold War. It briefly becomes a major force in post–World War II battles for civil rights for African Americans and for civil liberties for white and black labor-movement radicals before becoming a victim of Cold War anticommunism and government repression. William Patterson, former secretary of the ILD, led the group throughout its existence.

1949–1958   *The Smith Act Trials.* During the Smith Act trials, a series of prosecutions held from 1949 to 1958, leaders of the CPUSA are accused of violating the Smith Act, a 1940 statute that sets penalties for advocating the violent overthrow of the U.S. government. The prosecution argues that the CPUSA's policies promote violent revolution; the defendants counter that they advocate a peaceful transition to socialism and that the First Amendment's guarantee of free speech and association protects their membership in a political party. The trials lead to the U.S. Supreme Court decisions *Dennis v. United States* (1951) and *Yates v. United States* (1957).

B. D. Amis

B. D. Amis (1896–1993) is virtually unknown today and often over-looked by historians. As an African American Communist, he was a major figure in the black freedom struggle during the two decades between the world wars. At the time, the American Communist Party (CP) played a significant role in fighting for the rights of African Americans. This was especially true during CP's heyday in the late 1920s and the 1930s. In those years, Amis was, to be sure, part of the small circle of black radicals leading the struggle for workers' rights and racial justice. In 1930, Amis became the general secretary of the newly formed League of Struggle for Negro Rights and editor of its organ, The Liberator. *The league publicized the racial issues of the day, such as lynching, rallies, conferences, and picketing. Aptly described as "urbane in demeanor and a dynamic speaker," Amis was indeed one of the most important black activists of his time. His daughter, Debbie A. Bell, chairs the Eastern Pennsylvania/Delaware District of the CPUSA. B. D. Amis died in Virginia in 1993.*

■ ■ ■

Fond 515, Files of the Communist Party of the United States
in the Comintern Archives

The Negro National Oppression and
Social Antagonisms

The Communist, 1931

> "The Negro agricultural laborers and the tenant farmers feel
> most the pressure of the white persecution and exploitation.
> Thus the agrarian problem lies at the root of the Negro na-
> tional movement." (Thesis, Sixth World Congress.)

The Civil War, a struggle between the industrial bourgeoisie of the
North and the slave-owners of the South, did not achieve the real
emancipation of the slaves. It is true that by an amendment to the
federal constitution bourgeois democratic rights were granted, supposedly to guarantee the new freedom. For the first time the Negroes
were granted the right to vote, to hold public office, to obtain an
equal education, which for a brief period were enforced by Negro
militia and northern federal troops.

But the northern bourgeoisie entered into a rapprochement
with the overthrown southern plantation lords, thus deserting the
property-less former slaves. The northern capitalists were unable to
carry the bourgeois-democratic tasks of the war to the end, the taking of the land from the slave holders and giving it to the slaves. If
this had been done, the former slaves would not have been forced
to return to their former masters after their cowardly betrayal by the
northern bourgeoisie, to obtain a livelihood.

Thus the Negro masses in the South, left property-less by their
northern "friends," were abandoned to their fate at the hands of
their former masters. The former slave-holders soon denied the
Negroes their newly granted democratic rights and reduced them
to a state of semi-slavery, the plantation system.

Nominal slavery passed away, but the subsequent dependence
of the betrayed Negroes upon their previous masters continued
the institution in another form. The plantation tenancy system was
adopted by the landlords as a means to continue their robbery of
the Negro masses, and continued to the development of industrial
capital, in the North and South.

Repressive Measures

A way of securing peons is for an employer or his agent to go to a town or city and hire a group of laborers. He agrees to pay certain wages and transportation and provide the necessary provisions from the commissary, the company store. The laborers, indebted to their employer, trade out their meager wages at the company store. By false methods, trickery, and even foul play the employer keeps the peon in perpetual debt. What books are kept (by the planter only) have false entries. A peon with a large family is most desirable to the planter, who afforded a greater opportunity to increase his robbery of large numbers of permanent victims through his false bookkeeping system. Oft-times to assure that the peons do not attempt to run away, their children are taken from them.

To keep the peons on the plantations it is necessary to establish iron authority over them. The overseer is the terrorist of every plantation. He uses the whip and gun to strike terror among the peons, subjecting them to the will of the boss and slavery conditions. Women and children alike become the personal property of the white master. The latter grow up in ignorance, and the former are prostituted by the many white masters. By the use of sheer force these people are not allowed to leave the plantation, only on very rare occasions. If perchance a victim escapes, he is arrested under false pretexts, as jumping a contract, cheating, or false promises. Generally there is not a trial. But the officer returns the unfortunate peon to the plantation camp, where he is severely punished.

Convict Labor

Convict labor and the chain gang have resulted from peonage. The need of the South for a large supply of laborers has been used by as a pretext for the landlords to conscript men and women. A flimsy charge would place one in jail. Planters bargained with the courts for their prisoners, paying the fines, and putting many in involuntary servitude. By forced restraint and cooperation from constables, sheriffs, and other court officials, the prisoners released by the courts to the planters are kept in bondage and avenues of escape are closed. If one gets away, bloodhounds are put on his trail and when caught he is subjected to fiendish torture. Planters when brought before the courts on charges of peonage and using convict labor have answered that they had to whip Negroes brutally once in a while to keep them from rebelling.

The fact that there exist on the statute books of the federal government laws for prohibiting peonage does not safeguard the right of Negroes. This remnant of slavery, fastening its iron hold on upon millions of unfortunate victims, has its roots in a scoundrel social order whose dastardly rulers in their mad rush to amass riches out of the sweat and blood of the workers and peasants exploit and oppress the entire toiling class. The defenseless Negroes, considered as a caste of "untouchables," and who in the majority are agrarian workers, have not been liberated. Amendments to the present constitution will not free them. Only an agrarian revolution, with the proletariat assuming the hegemony under the leadership of Communists, will finally achieve freedom for this oppressed potential nation.

"It is a Yankee bourgeois lie to say that the yoke of slavery has been lifted in the United States."*

These social antagonisms (remnants of slavery) "stink of the disgusting atmosphere of the old slave market. This is downright robbery and slave-whipping barbarism at the peak of capitalist 'culture'."*

*Resolution of the Communist International on the *Negro Question in the United States.*

Fond 515, Files of the Communist Party of the United States in the Comintern Archives, Negro Bureau of the Comintern

Speech at the Thirteenth Plenum, CPUSA

September 1931

In the 20 minutes I have I want to deal with one point. And that is because the Party today is engaged in such a struggle that it is necessary that we must have the fullest clarification relative to the struggles we are conducting for Negro masses so that it may be turned into organizational results. No one will deny the fact that the Party has an overwhelming amount of influence among the Negro masses. This is best shown in their participation in the various demonstrations that the Party, the TUUL have held, also in the hunger marches and in the numerous other campaigns the Party has conducted. On August 1st, in the Party demonstrations against the war danger, here we can see a great upward trend in the number of participants of Negroes in the hundreds of demonstrations. For instance, in places like in the North, in Minnesota, etc., we see that these workers are not so very familiar with our systematic and energetic fight against the war danger, for the protection of the Soviet Union, but because of the correct approach of the Party, we were able to draw out large numbers to demonstrate. This influence of the Party has been the result of the Party beginning to conduct gigantic struggles in the fight for Negro rights. We have recorded positive achievements since the last Plenum. For instance, the Yokinen antiracist trial in New York which laid the very foundation for the absolute turn in our work in the Negro field.

The next large struggle was the developing of a large mass movement around the Scottsboro campaign and here, comrades, I want to dwell for quite a few moments, for the reason that in the Scottsboro campaign we have for the first time in the Party a gigantic struggle which has two aspects in the struggle for the Negro rights, the national questions and the class question.

Because of the united front policy we have carried on, we were able to mobilize hundreds of thousands of Negroes to participate in the building up of a mass defense movement in the Scottsboro campaign. However, because of the fact that we were able to win the mothers of all the boys to support us in this campaign, because we were able to mobilize thousands of Negro workers to help us build up this movement, we did not exploit these opportunities to the fullest extent.

The comrades did not understand the particular role of the Negro workers. For instance, when we decided to bring every mother to the North to conduct an energetic campaign in order to mobilize thousands of Negro workers to protest against the frameup, the comrades were not conscious of the necessity to pay special attention to the care of these mothers. I want to state that I believe that our comrades in Philadelphia do not receive our [Control Commission] directives if they don't read them. We were very careful when we knew we had in our hands a weapon which could become the sharpest instrument with which we could break down the illusions of the white liberals and petty-bourgeois reformist Negroes by utilizing these mothers to help build up this mass movement. In every district, however, we see looseness and a most criminal carelessness in the handling of the mothers.

In Philadelphia, we sent Mrs. Powell, the mother of the one of the boys. What did they do? We stated in our directive that these mothers must be placed with responsible Party comrades who should have the task of always and constantly guiding and watching over them. Mrs. Powell, however, was placed with the rankest sort of white chauvinist who put her to work washing dishes, scrubbing floors, washing duties, etc.

Now comrades, however, after the Philadelphia comrades have this deplorable situation drawn to their attention, some steps were made to correct this. But after Mrs. Powell was brought here to New York, where we take pride in having certain facilities to make these mothers more comfortable and help develop them, even here our comrades fell down on the job, placing her in an isolated home or rather a meeting hall in the most foul air and dirty quarters.

This shows what, comrades? First of all, that the comrades were not aware of the hazardous situation they placed us in. If our enemies would have found out that we handled the mothers like we did, what would have been the result? Take it the other way. If we knew these mothers were handled like this by the NAACP, would we not jump at their throats in meetings, conferences, etc.? Our comrades do not recognize that in dealing with the question, we have a special question and we cannot treat this question like we treat the ordinary question and like we treat the white workers. From now on, the comrades must recognize that in dealing with the Negro question they have a special task. And that is our task to show the Negro workers; yes, we are going to fight for their rights and to show them we are going to carry on an energetic campaign in order to prove that the things we put in writing will be carried out in practice. In the Camp Hill case, it was a result of our Scottsboro campaign, that the Negro peasants in Alabama were willing to carry on a campaign liking this case up with the Scottsboro case and other campaigns we were carrying on.

We noticed a decided lagging in this campaign. However, there was another campaign which proved a sort of a boomerang. The Chicago massacre and here we find a rise in the curve. The struggles that the comrades in Chicago conducted gave a little bit more of an impetus to the Scottsboro and the Camp Hill campaign.

Now as to some of the mistakes of the Scottsboro campaign. First I think we have to charge ourselves with making these mistakes and one of the crassest in my opinion in this campaign was when we started out to build block and neighborhood committees. Not that we should not have built them. This is the most effective way in which we could reach the masses by our united front from below, but we began to build block committees and neighborhood committees in certain districts and restricted and narrowed the base only to the issue of struggle to save the nine boys. This is not the correct policy. The policy should have been, and we did change afterwards, that the workers drawn into the block and neighborhood committees should not only be drawn into the struggle to save the nine Scottsboro boys, but that we should raise the level of their struggles, draw them into further political campaigns that we would develop their class-conscious and develop their moods for struggle against all forms of oppression and exploitation.

Another mistake and this was noticeable in almost every district. The comrades in trying to build united front movements from below followed in the trail of the Negro misleaders such as the NAACP and churches, going there and appealing to the "fair-play" of these misleaders and for them to appeal to "their" masses in the campaign. We would have built up a more genuine mass movement if we had absolutely ignored these misleaders and went about building the block and neighborhood committees and we would have drawn thousands more into the struggle than we did. Another mistake was the open arms with which we accepted one of the worst types of reactionary misleaders of the Negro masses, when [William] Pickens [the NAACP officer who was assigned to speak on the Scottsboro matter] wrote the International Labor Defense and sent them a few dollars endorsing the campaign, we came out with great big headlines welcoming Pickens into the struggle, stating that he had joined the struggle without exposing his reactionary role and without telling the masses that his action was caused not by his sincerity but by the mass pressure forcing him to take such a step. This we failed to do and this is a bad mistake. Closely connected with this was another serious mistake which I made myself and I want to take full responsibility for this. And this is the editorial which appeared in the *Liberator* last week where we also gave the crassest manifestation of Right wing opportunism in appealing to the bourgeois press to more energetically take up the struggle for Negro rights. I will not go into the details of what was the content of the editorial but it is sufficient to state that contents were of such character that there was a tendency to create false illusions among the Negro masses that they could rely of their Negro reformist leaders, that they would begin to struggle for their rights. Also that we somehow expected these petty-bourgeois reactionary newspaper leaders to use the columns of their press to expose the white terror and oppression and exploitation of the Negro masses. Another danger is that we did not link up the struggle of the Negro masses with the struggle of the white workers. And this brought into more sharp expression that in this appeal we absolutely distorted the role of the *Liberator*. And after we get through reading this editorial one would think that the Negro press will become an effective force to mobilize the Negro masses for struggle. Then there is no room for the *Liberator*?

Such mistakes hinder and hamper our struggle in mobilizing masses of Negro workers to participate in joint struggle with the workers and it is necessary at this time that whatever we put into the press, our policies, must be clear-cut decisive and correct.

Now comrades, in regard to the struggle today in the Negro field, some comrades have raised the question, because of these partial successes (and I want to state that in Chicago where they have had a partial success that they are now on the brink of the danger point). Here is a tremendous amount of influence built up among the Negro workers in the South side of Chicago and now we have an opportunity to show that we as a Communist Party, as a Bolshevik Party, can take this influence among the thousands of Negro workers and turn it into organizational gains and build our Party, that we can build our revolutionary unions, that we can build our LSNR, that we can build our *Liberator* into a mass organ. Unless we are able to realize some organizational results from this mass influence that we have in Chicago we will have to acknowledge that we are absolutely very weak, and the campaign will almost amount to naught. Some of the comrades realize the successes of these struggles of the share croppers in Alabama, because of the struggles in Chicago and Scottsboro, because of the militancy of the Negro workers in Birmingham in fighting police terror the comrades say they think it is time to raise a new perspective, whether we are in an insurrectionary period or not. We must have a new perspective.

We are not ready now to raise the question of a new perspective, neither are the Negro masses in a period of insurrection. Our task is to develop further the struggle of the Negro workers, economic struggles, political struggles, struggles for their day to day needs. Another task is to link up the struggles of the Negro masses with the struggles of the white proletariat. If we concern ourselves with these major tasks and develop the fighting political consciousness the next stage of their struggles will come and we will not have to worry about looking for it. To develop the struggles against the evictions, for immediate unemployment relief, against high rents, discrimination, terror and persecution, etc. is still our perspective for the present time, as well as developing joint struggles of the black and white workers.

Fond 515, Files of the Communist Party of the United States in the Comintern Archives

The National Recovery Act Lynch Drive
Calls for Mass Resistance

International Press Correspondence, February 9, 1934

The "New Deal" to the Negro masses was the same old deal in disguise. [National Recovery Administration] became the symbol, "Negro Repressive Act,"—"No Rights At All." In the industries that predominantly employ Negro workers, the N.R.A. operated in a repressive manner. Wage rates were generally omitted from the codes of "fair" labor competition in these industries. In the textile code the Negro unskilled laborer is classified as a cleaner or outside worker, thereby being excluded from the minimum wage provisions. According to an article in the September issue of the magazine, "Opportunity," three million Negro workers (domestics, personal servants, farm laborers, unskilled workers, etc.) are excluded entirely from the N.R.A. codes. In the codes that provide a minimum wage for Negroes, the differential is from 25 per cent to 50 per cent less. In the lumber code there is a wide disparity in the rates of wages paid to the Northern white lumber workers and those paid to the Negro lumber workers of the South. Frances Perkins, Secretary of Labor, admitting the open discriminatory practices of the N.R.A. states: "The low rates of twenty-five cents and twenty-seven cents per hour for the two Southern districts are presumably based on the predominance of Negro labor in those districts." To overcome such flagrant disparity, she gave the solution that the Negro must have "increased wages that will not unfairly compete with the wages of white laborers." This is the common practice of the federal government amongst Negro workers of the Federal Barge Line, operated by the War department. This strike in East St. Louis and St. Louis was against rotten working conditions of 12–15 hours per day, for which the men received pay for two hours' work. The N.R.A. Labor Board refused to give a hearing to the men; but the officials called the police who, through intimidation methods, tried to break the strike. During the application of the codes in the South, especially where there were wage increases, rather than give these increases to the Negro worker, the employer discharged him for the white worker.

The illusions in the "New Deal" among the Negro and white toilers were being shaken as the programme [sic] became a reality. Employment ceased; wages were cut; lay-offs set in; continued poverty and misery looked into the faces of the workers. Consequently there developed on the background of rapidly worsening conditions of the toilers a movement against the N.R.A. and its codes of "fair" competition for labor. This movement gained in momentum, as it swept every part of the country.

Naturally such wide disaffection took its sharpest form among the most exploited. To repel this deepening mass upsurge of Negro and white, which defied the dictates of the Mexican Federation of Labor officialdom and the government to harness it, the State and the employers, throwing caution to the winds, but under a well-prepared barrage of demagogy, let loose sharp and intensified and repressive measures against the toilers.

The Negro masses felt the full strength of the hammer blows of the growing reaction of the N.R.A. They did not only receive wage-cuts and were thrown out of jobs, but were attacked on every front. Lynchings increased in number and savageness. Over forty were lynched during the first year of the N.R.A. The Blue Eagle, emblem of the N.R.A., in a new wave of lynchings set out to crush with flame and torch, rope and gun, every bit of militant resistance of the Negro masses. Lynchings, legal and extralegal, received the sanction of employers and high State officials. They became holidays "in highly-cultured America" that recalled all the barbarous acts of the blackest days of the medieval period committed in the name of religion.

It was in this whipped-up lynch atmosphere that the lynch trails were set for the Scottsboro boys, and the legal lynching of Euel Lee took place. "Liberal" America, with Roosevelt at the helm of the "New Deal" ship, was determined to make the black man pay with his life for the misgivings of the N.R.A.

But the workers did not submit to this sharper terror easily. Under militant leadership, protests and struggles developed. The League of Struggle for Negro Rights issued a call for a nation-wide drive against lynchings and Negro oppression. The first united front regional conference against lynching was held in Baltimore, Maryland.

Baltimore is the home of the "liberal" democratic governor, Albert Ritchie, an ardent supporter of the N.R.A. It is close to the Eastern shore where George Armwood was lynched and burned to a chair by the elite citizens. These same people threatened to lynch the attorney of the International Labor Defense [I.L.D.], Bernard Ades, who very courageously defended Euel Lee. At the same time they asked to be allowed to supplant the courts, which in their opinion, were altogether too slow in legally lynching Lee. Ritchie openly stated that the mass resistance organized by the I.L.D., preventing the courts from rapidly carrying out the execution of Lee, was responsible for the mob heaping its hatred and vengeance in barbaric fashion on Armwood. Therefore "justice" must be served—

Lee must hang by his neck—there can be no further stay or reprieve of the sentence.

It was in such a setting that the public hearing and investigation of lynchings and Negro oppression and the anti-lynch conference were called. The purpose of the public hearing and inquiry was: (1) to collect factual material and documentary evidence of the flagrant discriminatory practices against the Negroes; (2) to show the economic cause for the super exploitation and oppression of the Negroes; (3) to assembly eye-witnesses to the Eastern shore lynchings and take their affidavits; (4) to receive investigators' reports on the new stages in the Scottsboro and Tuscaloosa cases; (5) to gather all of the available material and evidence a book similar to the Brown Book of the Hitler terror in Germany, with a similar title to "The Black Book of American Imperialism"; (7) to show the revolutionary way out.

The conference which immediately followed the hearing had its aims: (1) to launch a nation-wide drive against lynching under the leadership of the League of Struggle for Negro Rights and the International Labor Defense, building up the broadest kind of united front of joint actions; (2) to bring to the fore the programme [*sic*] of the L.S.N.R. in the struggle against national oppression; (3) to build the L.S.N.R. into a powerful mass organization; (4) to forge a mighty weapon out of the "Liberator" which should become the outspoken mouthpiece of the L.S.N.R. and the Negro people; (5) to show that only through revolutionary, only through the right of self-determination of the Negroes in the Black Belt could real freedom be achieved.

This immediate plan of action caused no little worry to the imperialists and their agents. They were aware of the deep dissatisfaction with the N.R.A. penetrating the Negro masses, especially discontent with the unequal wages established by the codes. They had before them the excellent response of the Negro class organizations. Therefore, these oppressors of the Negro people determined to defeat and sabotage the plan of action and attempt to smash the expanding influence of the Communist programme [*sic*] of liberation over the Negro people.

To accomplish such a slimy task, without creating consternation among the Negro people and white workers, the ruling class tried to proceed along concealed lines, using the "friends" of the Negroes to complete their deception. The arch supporter of Jim Crowism in Maryland and the hangman of Euel Lee, Governor Ritchie became the chief sponsor of a toothless anti-lynching Bill. Around the Governor and the Bill were grouped those betrayers of the struggles for Negro liberation, the National Association for the Advancement of Colored People and the Urban League; the white chauvinist apologists, the Socialist Party of Maryland. Previously the socialists had made a sham of asking that Ritchie should be impeached for his laxness in the Armwood lynching. But they withdrew from this position to support the lynchers of the Negro people. An attempt was made to draw the Negro masses into this false struggle. Extensive preparations were made to hold a mass meeting on the anti-lynching Bill to be presented to the Maryland legislature. After issuing thousands of leaflets, utilizing the press and pulpit, and conducting a campaign of shameful slander and lies against the L.S.N.R. and the I.L.D., the true defenders of the rights of Negro people, the meeting was held. But only 125 people responded to their frenzied efforts.

In contrast to this, the L.S.N.R. and the I.L.D., with considerable help from the Communist Party, mobilized the trade unions, certain locals of the A.F. of L., Negro organizations, unemployed organizations, and individuals for a united front and a minimum programme [sic] of action. At the same time the treacherous acts of the Negro misleaders and their white liberal friends were exposed. The response was good. The public inquiry in the New Albert Hall drew a capacity crowd of 2,000 paid admissions. To the conference over 700 delegates were elected from New York, New Jersey, Connecticut, Philadelphia, Baltimore, Washington, D.C. and the Eastern shore. Steel workers, dock workers, employed and unemployed, Negro and white, sincere intellectuals, professionals, members from the N.A.A.C.P. local, Negro lodges and churches were delegates.

The revolutionary programme [sic] of the L.S.N.R., the struggle for equal rights of the Negroes in the North and for self-determination of the Negro majority in the Black Belt, was accepted as the only way to beat back the attacks of the white ruling class by the overwhelming majority of the delegates. The speeches of rank and file workers told of their willingness to join a fighting united front, rejecting the legal pussy-footing programme [*sic*] of the reformists. These workers gave the assurance of carrying the L.S.N.R. plan of action back to their organizations to help build up the drive against Negro oppression.

At the inquiry a large tribunal of judges, composed of workers, intellectuals and professionals was elected. Eyewitnesses from the Eastern shore spoke. Evidence was introduced by investigators from the Tuscaloosa and Scottsboro cases. Before the eyes of an aroused working class and Negro people were unfolded the atrocities of American imperialism and its "New Deal" for the Negro masses. The indictment of the guilty for the long history of subjugation and humiliation, for the brutal oppression of a whole nation and for the new wave of lynching was thrust into the face of the white ruling class. The conference and the hearing threw out the challenge to mobilize mass resistance; to fight against Negro oppression.

Outstanding among the shortcomings were: (1) an underestimation of the tremendous response, in spite of poor preparations, to the hearing and the conference which called for revolutionary struggle against Negro persecution; (2) insufficient work done by the Communist workers, especially in the New York district, to penetrate A.F. of L. locals, working-class organizations and the new Negro organizations; (3) failure to answer the question of delegates concretely how they can work alone after returning home to carry out the fight against Negro oppression; (4) lack of preparations and popularizing of the *Liberator* and sale of the pamphlet containing the programme [*sic*] and manifesto of the L.S.N.R.

These mistakes must be corrected in the conferences which are to be held in Chicago, Cleveland, St. Louis, etc.

American imperialism and its new disguise, the "New Deal," the N.R.A., shall not go unchallenged in its grinding under its iron heel of oppression the Negro nation. It shall be met with stubborn resistance and working-class determination in battle, with mass mobilization of the Negro people and white workers, fighting for land, equality and freedom for a nation of 12,000,000 Negroes under the yoke of American imperialism.

Harry Haywood

As a principal figure in the American Communist movement, Harry Haywood (1898–1985) stands out as a key theorist on the controversial "national question" of African Americans in the United States. In this role, he was a sharp Marxist critic of middle-class black "reformers" found in the National Association for the Advancement of Colored People and in the field of black journalism.

An exceptional young black intellectual, Haywood Hall Jr. joined the American Communist Party in 1925 and took "Harry Haywood" as his party pseudonym. He had, in fact, commenced his revolutionary vocation in 1922 when he enrolled in the African Blood Brotherhood. Soon afterward, he joined the Young Communist League and subsequently journeyed to Moscow, where he studied at the Communist University of the Toilers of the East and at the International Lenin School. A talented radical theorist, Haywood focused on the issue of the political status of African Americans in the American racial caste system that had developed after the end of Reconstruction. Likewise, he dealt with the development of the Native Republic Thesis for the South African Communist Party. Haywood played a significant part in composing the Comintern's "Resolutions on the Negro Question" in 1928 and 1930. In a clever use of the Marxist dialectical method, he cogently argued that in the Black Belt of the American South, African Americans formed an "oppressed nation" with the right to "self-determination."

During the heyday of American communism in the 1930s, Haywood emerged as a national leader in the American Communist movement. Indeed, he served on the party's Central Committee (1927–1938) and in the Politburo (1931–1938). He also participated in the major factional scuffles within the CPUSA that involved the struggles centering on Jay Lovestone, Earl Browder, and William Z. Foster. Furthermore, in 1935 he led the "Hands Off Ethiopia" campaign in Chicago's black South Side to oppose Italy's invasion of Ethiopia, and when the eleven major Communist leaders stood trial in 1949 under the Smith Act, Haywood carried out the assignment of research for the defense.

▪ ▪ ▪

Fond 515, Files of the Communist Party of the United States in the Comintern Archives, Negro Bureau of the Comintern

Report to the Eighth Convention of the Communist Party of the U.S.A., Cleveland, Ohio

The Tasks of the Communist Party in Winning Working Class Leadership of the Negro Liberation Struggles, and the Fight against Reactionary Nationalist-Reformist Movements among the Negro People

April 2–8, 1934

Negro Reformism: Agent of U.S. Imperialism

Comrade Browder in his excellent report outlined in the clearest fashion the position of the Party on the Negro question, and laid the basis for a correct approach to our task in work among Negroes in the present period. Comrade Browder stressed the importance of the fight on two fronts against white chauvinism as the main danger and against petty bourgeois nationalism, which he correctly called the "reverse side of white chauvinism."

In my report I wish to elaborate on this question of the fight on two fronts, particularly in relation to the fight against the Negro reformist danger, which, in the present period, has become acute and menacing.

An outstanding characteristic of the present moment is the sharp increase in the activities of the Negro bourgeois reformists and petty bourgeois nationalist leaders among the Negro masses. We find that these activities have not only been intensified, but are assuming more varied and subtle forms. In addition to the official bourgeois reformist organizations and their activities, there has appeared upon the scene in the recent period numerous petty bourgeois nationalist movements. We also witness definite attempts to crystallize "Left" reformist Negro movements.

This phenomenon is directly connected with the sharpening class struggle and growing radicalization of the Negro toilers. Only on this basis can it be explained. We might say that the increased activities of the Negro reformists, their attempts to strengthen nationalism among the masses, take place in direct proportion to the increase of our revolutionary influence among the Negro masses. We see that wherever we begin serious work among the Negroes, wherever our influence is extended among them, we find ourselves confronted sharply with the problem of the struggle against Negro reformist as an immediate obstacle in the revolutionization of the Negro masses, as for example, in Chicago, in St. Louis, the South, in connection with the Scottsboro campaign and the struggle against lynching. Everywhere, Negro reformists and petty bourgeois nationalist leaders of all shades, under the cover of the most cunning demagogy, are feverishly working.

What is the object of these activities? It is clear that their object is to halt the growing revolutionary drift of the Negro masses, to hinder the growing unity of Negro and white toilers in the struggle against rising fascist reaction, to hold the masses under the influence of bourgeois reformism, petty bourgeois nationalism, which means objectively, to hold them to the shackles of imperialism. It is now becoming clearer than ever that Negro reformism is the main enemy within the ranks of the Negro people, the chief social support of imperialist Jim-Crow reaction among the Negro masses. Therefore, the struggle against and exposure of the Negro reformists and the petty bourgeois nationalist leaders, their isolation from the masses, is a central, most urgent task of our Party and the revolutionary movement at the present time. Involved in this fight for the liberation of the masses from the treacherous influences of the Negro reformists and their organizations, is the whole question of proletarian hegemony and party leadership in the rising national revolutionary movement of the Negro people. It is a question of who will beat whom. What policy shall prevail? Our proletarian class policy of a revolutionary alliance between the Negro masses and the white working class for the overthrow of American imperialism and the realization of the rights of Negroes or the reformist policy of surrender to imperialism, the policy which substitutes reactionary utopian illusions in place of revolutionary struggle, a policy which can lead only to defeat, and to strengthening the yoke of imperialist oppression upon the masses of Negro toilers and the white toilers as well?

The Object of Negro Reformism

Let us examine some of the activities of the Negro bourgeois reformists, petty bourgeois nationalist organizations in the present situation. Among the Negro reformist organizations we find the chief role is still allotted to the National Association for the Advancement of Colored People. In the leadership of this organization, we find Negro bourgeois reformists of the type of Walter White, Pickens, Schuyler, Du Bois en bloc, with white liberals ("enlightened" imperialist elements) of the type of Joel Spingarn, Mary White Ovington, etc., and even outspoken imperialist politicians such as Senator Arthur Capper, Governor General Murphy of the Philippines, etc.; also open Negro reactionaries of the type of Dr. Robert Moton of Tuskegee. It is these imperialist elements that govern the policies of the organization. The composition of the leadership of the N.A.A.C.P. thus gives a clear indication of this policy.

What is this policy?

The guiding theory on which the policy is based is that: The Negro question can be solved within the confines of the present capitalist imperialist social order without revolutionary struggle. That the fate of the Negro masses is bound up with the maintenance of capitalism, or as Kelly Miller, outspoken Negro conservative expresses it: "Capital is the Negro's friend; white labor is his enemy." Therefore, according to this, the winning of Negro rights does not entail a fight against capital, i.e., imperialism; on the contrary, it implies the collaboration with the white imperialist rulers, or in the words of the N.A.A.C.P. leaders, "united front of the 'best' elements of both races." Against whom? Against the rising mass movement of Negro and white toilers, particularly against its leaders—the Communists.

This is the core of Negro bourgeois reformism. From this flows its tactical line of reliance on bourgeois courts, legislative bodies, its treacherous compromises with the white ruling courts, legislative bodies, its treacherous compromises with the white ruling class, its reactionary sabotage of the revolutionary struggles for Negro rights. "The Constitution is the ship, all else is the sea," says Kelly Miller.

In the present period of sharpening class struggles and political awakening of the Negro peoples, this policy implies the active supplementing of the ruling class tactic of split and division in the ranks of the working class; it implies active alliance with all reactionary forces against the rising national liberation movement of the Negro masses, against the revolutionary labor movement, and its leaders, the Communist Party. Negro reformism has become an active agent of the ruling imperialist bourgeoisie in helping to prepare the way for fascism. . . .

Earl Browder Papers, Special Collections Research Center, Syracuse University Library

The Struggle for the Leninist Position on the Negro Question in the U.S.A.

The Communist, 1933

The present program of our Party on the Negro question was first formulated at the Sixth Congress of the Communist International, in 1928. On the basis of the most exhaustive consideration of all the conditions of the Negro people in the United States as well as the experience of the Party in its work among Negroes, that Congress definitely established the problem of the Negroes as that of an oppressed nation among whom there existed all the requisites for the national revolutionary movement against American imperialism.

This estimation was a concrete application of the Marxist-Leninist conception of the national question to the conditions of the Negroes and was predicated upon the following premises: first, the concentration of the large masses of Negroes is in the agricultural regions of the Black Belt, where they constitute a majority of the population; secondly, the existence of powerful relics of the former chattel slave system in the exploitation of the Negro toilers—the plantation system based on sharecropping, landlord supervision of crops, debt slavery, etc.; thirdly, the development, on the basis of these slave remnants, of a political superstructure of inequality expressed in all forms of social proscription and segregation; denial of civil rights, right to the franchise, to hold public offices, to sit on juries, as well as in the laws and customs of the South. This vicious system is supported by all forms of arbitrary violence, the most vicious being the peculiar American institution of lynching. All of this finds its theoretical justification in the imperialist ruling class theory of the "natural" inferiority of the Negro people.

This whole vicious system of oppression, while being most sharply felt by the Negro masses in the South also affects their social status in the rest of the country. The Negro poor farmers and the farm laborers fleeing from the misery and starvation of the Southern plantations to the industrial centers of the North, do not thereby obtain freedom. On the contrary, at their heels follows also the heritage of plantation slavery resulting in lower wages, worse living conditions, discrimination in social life even in the "liberal" North.

Thus the agrarian revolution, i.e. the struggle of the poverty-stricken and land-starved Negro sharecroppers and poor farmers in the Black Belt and in the South for the land, for the destruction of all vestiges of slave bondage—this, together with the general struggle for democratic rights of the Negro people all over the country, as well as for their rights to independent national existence in the Black Belt, constitutes the chief axis of the Negro national liberation movement in the U.S.A.

The enslavement of the Negro masses in the United States is an important prop of American imperialism. American imperialism is fundamentally interested in the preservation of the slave remnants in Southern agriculture and the national oppression of the Negro people as a condition for the extraction of super profits. It is the force that stands behind the Southern white ruling classes (capitalists and landlords) in their direct and violent plunder of the Negro masses in the Black Belt. Therefore, the liberation struggles of the Negro masses are directed against the very foundation of the capitalist-imperialist social structure in the United States.

In the present epoch of imperialism and proletarian revolution the Negro question in the United States must be conceived as part of the national colonial problem, or, in other words, it is part of the general world-wide problem of freedom of the oppressed and dependent peoples from the shackles of imperialism.

The Leninist conception of the national question in the present historical epoch was formulated with remarkable clarity by Comrade Stalin in his book *The Foundations of Leninism*:

> It (the national question) is now seen to be the world-wide problem of the Deliverance of the inhabitants of the colonial and dependent countries from the yoke of imperialism. . . . The imperialist war and the Russian Revolution have confirmed the Leninist view that the national problem can only be solved in the arena of the proletarian revolution; that *for the revolution of the western world the path of victory lies by the way of revolutionary alliance with the struggle of colonial and dependent nationalities to throw off the yoke of imperialism.* The national question is part of the general question of the proletarian revolution, part of the question of the dictatorship of the proletariat.
>
> This Leninist treatment of the national question applies with full force to the Negro problem in the United States.
>
> This question, which prior to and during the Civil War and Reconstruction was a part of the bourgeois revolution, now becomes part of the proletarian revolution. The proletarian revolution must solve in passing the uncompleted task of the bourgeois democratic and agrarian revolution in the South, left over by the Civil War.
>
> A radical transformation of the agrarian structure of the Southern States is one of the basic tasks of the revolution. . . . Only the victorious proletarian revolution will completely and finally solve the agrarian and national questions

of the Southern United States in the interest of the overwhelming majority of the Negro population in the country.
(Thesis of the Sixth Congress of the C[ommunist] I[nter-
national] on the Revolutionary Movement in the Colonies.)

The Negro masses, once the allies of the Northern bourgeoisie
(during the Civil War and Reconstruction), have now become the
allies of the proletariat. In their struggle for national liberation these
masses constitute an important part of the army of the revolutionary
proletariat in the struggle for the overthrow of American capitalism.
Hence, the victory of the proletarian revolution in the United States
and the struggle of the Negro masses for national liberation demand
the consummation of a united fighting front of the white toilers and
the Negro people against the common enemy,—American imperialism. Such a united front can only be effective on the basis of direct
and effective support by the white working class (as the working
class of the oppressor nation) to the efforts of the Negro masses to
free themselves from the imperialist yoke. In this connection it is
important to keep in mind the dictum of Karl Marx to the English
working class on the Irish question: "A people which oppresses
another people cannot itself be free."

From this Marxist-Leninist formulation of the Negro question
proceeds the line of the Party. While fighting against all forms of
inequality of the Negro people, for the abolition of all forms of slave
exploitation and oppression and for complete social equality, the
Party was urged by the Sixth Congress of the Communist International to come forward openly and unreservedly for the rights of
Negroes in the Black Belt to national self-determination. The mobilization of the masses of toilers for this struggle was to go hand in
hand with a pitiless fight against all forms of white chauvinism (the
ideology of the imperialist oppressor) as the main danger, while at
the same time all hangovers of petty bourgeois nationalist distrust
among the Negro toilers were to be patiently combated.

Only on this basis could there be welded a close, unbreakable
unity between the Negro and white toilers in their struggle against
the common enemy. Only in this way could our Party fulfill its international proletarian obligations. Such were the directives of the Sixth
Congress on the Negro question in the U.S.A.

This treatment of the Negro question as a question of an oppressed nation was, however, by no means new. Lenin, in his writings on this question had already laid the theoretical ground work for our Negro program. As early as 1913, in his brochure *The Development of Capitalism in American Agriculture,* Lenin, in his defending of the Marxist position on the agrarian question against the theorists of the Narodniki (populists) and Social Revolutionaries, laid bare the agrarian essence of the Negro question, indicating its national revolutionary character. In reply to the petty-bourgeois economist, Himmer, who contended that the "United States was a country which never knew feudalism and is foreign to its economic survivals," Lenin wrote: "This statement is in direct opposition to the truth, for the survivals of slavery differ in no way from the survivals of feudalism and the survivals of slavery are very strongly felt up to the present time in the former slave-owning South."

In the same pamphlet Lenin compared the position of the Negroes in the South with that of the serfs in Czarist Russia, stating that the "similarity of the economic position of the Negroes with that of the former serfs in the agrarian centers of Russia is remarkable. . . .The South," Lenin continued, "is a hemmed-in prison with the absence of fresh air for the 'liberated' Negroes."

It was on the basis of the analysis that the Second Congress of the Communist International placed the Negro question in the U.S.A. as the problem of an oppressed nation. In the thesis of this Congress on the national and colonial question which was developed under the direct guidance of Lenin, the Communist Parties were committed to "support the revolutionary movement *among subject nations (for example, Ireland, American Negroes and in the colonies)*" [emphasis added—H.H.].

The revolutionary program of the Party on the Negro question has been tested and confirmed in the development of the class struggle in the U.S.A. and in some substantial political gains for the Party in the leadership of the Negro masses.

Although the Party from its very inception raised the slogan of struggle for Negro rights, its activities in this field did not result in any real success in the leadership of mass struggle among Negros. Obviously, this was in the main due to our theoretical unclarity, our lack of a real Leninist approach to the Negro question as a question of an oppressed nation. Consequently the work of the Party during this period was fraught with many errors and weaknesses. Without waging an uncompromising fight for the emancipation of the Negroes as a nation, for their right to national self-determination in the Black Belt, without bringing forward the historical connection between the struggle and that of the white working class, it was impossible to a conduct a consistent fight against the poisonous influences of white chauvinism in the ranks of the white working class and to overcome distrust among the Negro toilers. Without the recognition of this right, it was impossible to weld the iron unity of the working class, to develop its hegemony and the leadership of the Party in the liberation struggles of the Negro toilers.

It was this lack of Leninist clarity on the question of self-determination that prevented the Party from exciting any appreciable influence upon the first great movement of Negro masses since the Civil War and the Reconstruction period. This potentially revolutionary movement of the Negro toilers, which arose in the post-war period, was allowed to fall under the influence of reactionary petty-bourgeois utopians led by Marcus Garvey and thereby diverted from a struggle against American imperialism into channels of a "peaceful return to Africa."

These dangerous weaknesses in our work among Negros could only be overcome on the basis of the development of a real Bolshevik Leninist program, the kernel of which is the conception of the Negro question as that of an oppressed nation, as part of the question of the proletarian revolution. Only on this basis could the party effect a decisive change in its Negro work and come forward as the real leader in the struggle of the Negro masses against imperialism. This program was a great contribution to the class struggle of the American working class, giving it a powerful weapon with which to break through the barriers of bourgeois race and national hatred, to tap the tremendous reserve force of the proletariat, the struggle of the Negro masses against imperialist oppression, and to reunite the Negro and white toilers in a common struggle against capitalism.

The first real achievements of our Party in the leadership of the struggles of the Negro masses date from the beginnings of the application of this Leninist line. A historic landmark in the development of our Negro work was the public trial of August Yokinen. In this trial the case of discrimination by a white Party member against Negroes was made the occasion for a political demonstration in which the Party's program on the Negro question and the struggle against white chauvinism were dramatized with an unprecedented effect before the widest masses throughout the country. Comrade Browder in his report before American students, in estimating the political significance of this trial declared "that it was a public challenge dramatically flung into the face of one of the basic principles of social relationships in America—the American institution of Jim Crowism. . . . The expulsion of Yokinen expressing our declaration of war against white chauvinism exerted a tremendous influence to draw the Negro masses closer to us."

In this trial the Party achieved a great step forward in the education of its membership and the masses around the Party on our program on the Negro question. This was particularly exemplified in Comrade Yokinen himself who, after six months, came back into the Party as one of the staunchest fighters for its program of Negro liberation and who, as a result of his courageous and militant stand on this question, was deported by the Negro-hating imperialist government. The trial of Yokinen served to prepare the Party ideologically for a real interest in the struggle for Negro rights.

The Yokinen trial was immediately followed by the organization of a mass movement to save the lives of the Scottsboro boys. On the basis of the political preparation through the Yokinen trial the Party was able to seize effectively upon the issue of the frame-up of these boys to develop a tremendous campaign of mass action and the exposure of the whole system of national oppression of the Negroes. The Scottsboro campaign marked the first real nationwide mobilization of masses by the Party for a concrete struggle against one of the cornerstones of capitalist Negro oppression—the institution of lynching. Through the struggle on this issue the Party was able to bring its program before the widest masses of Negro and white toilers, arousing among them the greatest sympathy and confidence. Scottsboro, as the first big battle conducted by the Party on the front of Negro national liberation, did much to break down the traditional barriers of chauvinism and national distrust separating the Negro and white toilers. This struggle, which was coupled with

a real political exposure of the treacherous role of the Negro bourgeois reformists of the N.A.A.C.P., hastened the process of class
differentiation among the Negros—the separation of the interests
of the Negro proletarian and semi-proletarian masses from the general interests of "race solidarity" as propagated by the Negro bourgeois nationalists. The Negro toilers began to understand class divisions. They began to find out who their friends were and who their
enemies.

Only though the vigorous application of our correct Leninist
program on the Negro question could the Party carry through and
lead such a struggle as the Scottsboro campaign. This campaign
gave rise to the sudden movement of mass participation of Negro
workers on an unprecedented scale in the general struggles of the
working class throughout the country. The great strike of the Pennsylvania, Ohio and West Virginia coal miners which broke out in
1931, during the first part of the Scottsboro campaign, witnessed
greater participation of Negro workers than any other economic
action led by the revolutionary trade unions. Large masses of the
Negro workers rallied to the unemployed movement, displaying
matchless militancy in the actions of the unemployed. Notable
examples of this were the heroic demonstrations against evictions
in the Negro neighborhoods of Chicago and Cleveland.

While the Negro masses were beginning to participate more
and more in the class struggles in the North, an event of great historical significance occurred in the Black Belt—the organization of
the Sharecroppers Union and the heroic resistance of the sharecroppers to the attacks of the landlords and sheriffs at Camp Hill,
Alabama. In this struggle, the revolutionary ferment of the Negro
poor farmers and sharecroppers received its first expression, resulting in the establishment of the first genuine revolutionary organization among the Negro poor farmers—the militant Sharecroppers
Union. The agrarian movement of the Negro masses was further
continued and developed in the Tallapoosa fight in which the sharecroppers gave armed resistance to the legalized robbery of the landlords and merchants.

This whole series of class and national liberation struggles was
further deepened and politicized through the Communist presidential election campaign of 1932. In this campaign the Party was able

to further extend its program among the masses, rallying large numbers of Negros behind its political slogans.

Thus the application of the Bolshevik program in conditions of sharpening crisis and growing radicalization of the Negroes has resulted in the extension of the political influence of the Party among broad masses of Negros, and in the growth of the Party membership among them. Of outstanding importance in this period is the establishment of the Party in the South and in the Black Belt.

These struggles have led to a growing class consciousness of the Negro working class and its emergence upon the political arena as an independent class force in the Negro liberation movement. In the course of these struggles the Negro working class is rapidly liberating itself from the treacherous reformist influences. Thus the characteristic of the present stage of development of the Negro movement is the maturing of this important driving force of Negro liberation—the Negro industrial working class. The Negro workers, in close organic unity with the white working class and under the leadership of the Communist Party are the only force capable of rallying the masses of Negro toilers in a victorious struggle against capitalism. The struggle for Negro liberation is now taking place under conditions of growing proletarian hegemony and Communist Party leadership.

The Negro question at the present time assumes greater significance than at any time since the Civil War and Reconstruction period. The present period marks for the first time the participation of masses of Negroes in the political life of the country as a force independent of the major capitalist parties. The significance of the Negro question as a factor in the sharpening of the revolutionary crisis of America imperialism has been thereby greatly increased.

The Leninist line on the Negro question was hammered out in the sharpest struggle against the opportunist line developed under the leadership of [Jay] Lovestone. In the period prior to the Sixth Congress of the C.I. the work of the Party was characterized by weakness and hesitancy. This was due to the absence of a Leninist line on this question. These dangerous shortcomings of the Party in its work among Negroes were not at first so much expressed in open theoretical formulations, as they were expressed in practice characterized by neglect, passivity and indifference.

However, it remained for Lovestone to provide theoretical foundation for all the opportunist views prevalent in the Party on the Negro question and to crystallize them into a definite right wing line in which all weaknesses were justified. This line was an integral part of the whole system of right wing views put forward in the Party by Lovestone, which found its fruition in the counterrevolutionary theory of American exceptionalism. This line was first clearly formulated in the report of Lovestone at the Fifth Convention of our Party (1927). In this report Lovestone stated the following:

The migration of hundreds of thousands of Negroes from the South into the industrial centers of the North and East is rapidly changing the Negro masses from a reserve of capitalist reaction into a reserve of the proletarian revolution.

In other words, as long as the Negros remained on the farms in the South they were reserves of capitalist reaction and could be considered reserves of the proletarian revolution only to the extent that they migrated into the industrial centers of the North. It is clear that this formulation justifies the complete desertion of the Negro toilers of the South. At the same time it rejects the role of the Negro peasantry as allies of the proletarian revolution and as an essential driving force, under the leadership of the Negro industrial working class, in the Negro liberation movement. This whole line was based upon a social-democratic denial of the national agrarian question among Negroes.

Not only did the Lovestoneites deny the possibility of revolutionary struggle on the part of the Negroes. In the South they considered the very existence of the Negro agricultural masses as inimical to such struggles.

This counter-revolutionary conception was categorically rejected in the resolution of the Sixth Congress of the C.I. and in the resolution of the Executive Committee of the Communist International of October 26, 1928. Thus the agrarian problem lies at the roots of the Negro national movement. The great majority of the Negroes in the rural districts of the South are *'not reserves of capitalist reaction' but potential allies of the revolutionary proletariat* [emphasis added—H.H.]. Their objective position facilitates their transformation into a revolutionary force which under the leadership of the proletariat will be able to participate in the joint struggles with all other workers against capitalist exploitation.

The theory of the Negro masses in the South as "reserves of capitalist reaction" attained its further development in the Lovestone–Pepper theory of the Industrial Revolution in the South. The "Industrial Revolution in the South" was a cornerstone of the whole system of opportunist views which comprised the theory of American exceptionalism.

According to this theory American capitalism was to find a way out of growing contradictions and escape the general crisis of world capitalism through the opening up of a whole new territory for capitalist expansion—the Southern states. This was to be done through the establishment of industries, and the mechanization of agriculture.

Thus the perspective was not one of the inevitable sharpening of the crisis in the U.S.A. but the opening up of a new era of unlimited prosperity for American capitalism, the ushering in of a "Hooverian Age" corresponding to the Victorian Age of British capitalism. Thus in America we were confronted not with decaying, moribund capitalism but progressive, robust capitalism. This counter-revolutionary movement of the theories of the bourgeois liberal apologists and enthusiasts reflected the awe of the petty bourgeoisie before the strength and "impregnability" of American imperialism.

On the Negro question this theory represented a continuation and further development of the theory of the Negro masses as a "reserve of capitalist reaction." The "industrial revolution" was to sweep away the remnants of slavery in Southern agriculture, proletarianize the Negro peasantry and thus automatically disentangle the complicated problem of national antagonism in the South. The Negro question as a special national question was to be solved within the confines of the capitalist imperialist structure without a struggle.

The whole opportunist theory of American exceptionalism was shattered in the Address of the Communist International to the C.P.U.S.A. (May 1929), which reads in part:

> With distinctness unprecedented in history, American capitalism is exhibiting now the effects of the inexorable laws of capitalist development, the laws of decline and downfall of

capitalist society. The general crisis of capitalism is growing more rapidly than it may seem at first glance. The crisis will shake also the foundations of American imperialism.

In refuting Lovestone's views on the Negro question the C.I. Resolution of 1930 reads:

> . . . the prospect for the future is not an inevitable dying away of the national revolutionary Negro movements in the South, as Lovestone prophesized, but on the contrary a great advance of this movement and the rapid approach of the revolutionary crisis in the Black Belt.

Resistance to the C.I. program on the Negro question was further continued after the Sixth Congress in Pepper's slogan, "Negro Soviet Republics." This was an attempt on the part of Lovestone and Pepper to smuggle in the old opportunist line of denial of the Negro nationalist agrarian question under the left phrases. In effect it amounted to making the acceptance of Soviets by the Negro masses in the Black Belt a condition of the Party's support of their struggle for the right of self-determination. This imposition of the slogan of Soviets from above on the Negro masses was equivalent to dictating to the Negro toilers the forms in which they must conduct their struggles against imperialism and consequently negated the whole principle of the right of self-determination. Also the slogan of a "Soviet Republic" contained an opportunist attempt to skip over the present stage of preparation and organization of the Negro masses in the struggle for their immediate demands for the right of self-determination. This opportunist distortion of Pepper's was definitely rejected in the C.I. Resolution which states:

> Moreover, the Party cannot make its stand for this slogan dependent upon any conditions, even the condition that the proletariat has the hegemony in the national revolutionary Negro movement or that the majority of the Negro population in the Black Belt adopts the Soviet form (as Pepper demanded), etc.

The theory of the Negro masses in the South as "reserves of capitalist reaction," made its last open stand in the bourgeois liberal conception which regarded the Negro question not as a national question but as a race question. This conception gained ground among some Party comrades after the Sixth Congress and served to cloak their resistance to the line of the C.I. and the Party.

According to these comrades the Negro question arises solely from racial distinctions and their utilization by the bourgeoisie. In this they failed to see the profound social antagonisms which lie at the base of the Negro problem, i.e., the agrarian question and the struggle for democratic rights. Consequently the movement of the Negro toilers is reduced to a feeble bourgeois liberal opposition against race prejudice as divorced from its economic and social roots. It is clear that such a theory is nothing but a capitulation to bourgeois liberalism. This dangerous distortion of our line on the Negro question was categorically rejected by the C.I. and the Party. In this regard the Resolution of the C.I., October, 1930, while recognizing the role of the race factor in the oppression of the Negroes, definitely states:

> The Negro question in the United States must be viewed from the standpoint of its peculiarity, namely, as the question of an *oppressed nation,* which is in a peculiar and extraordinarily distressing situation of national oppression not only in view of the prominent *racial distinctions* (marked difference in the color of skin, etc.), but above all because of considerable *social antagonism* (remnants of slavery).

At the bottom of these anti-Bolshevik theories on the Negro question lies a deep-rooted underestimation of the Negro liberation movement as a powerful force in the sharpening of the revolutionary crisis of American imperialism and consequently the nonunderstanding of this movement as an integral part of the proletarian revolution.

Only on the basis of the sharpest struggle against and the defeat of these anti-Leninist conceptions within its ranks has the Party been able to go forward in the winning of the Negro masses.

Although it can be said generally that our Party has rallied to the struggle against the worst manifestations of these errors that have been so harmful to our work in the past it must be said that survivals of these anti-Leninist ideas still persist, retarding the development of our work among Negroes. While the Party has become a real factor in the struggle for Negro rights and its political influence is rapidly increasing among ever larger sections of the Negro toilers, these successes are by no means commensurate with the objective possibilities and the rising upsurge of the masses. We are still lagging behind the rapidly deepening ferment among the Negro toilers. Our movement among Negroes still lacks a solid organizational base in the shops, factories and in the neighborhoods. This is noticeable first of all in the extremely high turnover in the Negro membership of the Party, in the relatively small number of Negro workers in our revolutionary trade unions, and in the insufficient bringing forward of Negro cadres in all phases of Party work. There are still grave weaknesses in our struggle against and exposure of the Negro bourgeois reformist leadership. These weaknesses were brought out in the united front on the Scottsboro campaign immediately following the Decatur verdict. In this united front there were manifested open opportunist tendencies in the direction of capitulation to the Negro reformists as well as right sectarian tendencies which would narrow down the united front. In the struggle against white chauvinism there is to be observed a widespread tendency to replace a consistent and daily struggle for the specific demands of the masses of white toilers in the struggle for the specific demands of the Negro masses by occasional spectacular anti-chauvinist demonstrations in the form of mass trials, which in most cases were badly prepared. In connection with the struggles for Negro rights there is noticeable an inability to connect up the popularization of our full program on the Negro question with the development of partial struggle for the daily needs of the Negro masses in the shops, factories, neighborhood and on the plantations.

While the Party has carried through energetically general campaigns on national liberation issues as witnessed in the Scottsboro campaign and the Communist election struggles, nevertheless these general struggles have not been sufficiently utilized for the development of local struggles, for the mobilization of Negro toilers in the shops, factories and neighborhoods and on the plantations in the struggle for their most vital needs. Our weaknesses in the development of the struggles of the Negro toilers on the economic field are most glaringly manifested in the work of the revolutionary trade unions. The directives of the Fourteenth Plenum which call for making the Red unions the "real channels of Negro work" have not been sufficiently understood by the Party.

These shortcomings in our work among Negros arise from two sources—first, they are connected with the general weakness of the Party as characterized in the Open Letter to the Extraordinary Party Conference. These are the failure to carry through a real Bolshevik policy of concentration of our work on the most important industries and factories and among the decisive sections of the American working class. Inasmuch as the main masses of Negro workers are also concentrated on the decisive industries of the country—coal, steel, marine—this lack of a concentration policy must necessarily affect the work of organization of the Negro working class. Second, an analysis of the shortcomings of our Party will also show that they are to a considerable extent traceable to the still existing lack of clarity in regard to the Leninist conception of the Negro question as a national question, i.e., failure to understand this question as essentially a question of allies for the proletarian revolution. This is expressed in a denial of the necessity for a special approach to the Negro workers, a tendency to blur over their special demands, failure to raise them. This is most glaringly expressed in our trade union and shop work as well as to some extent in the field of unemployment. A prevalent tendency in our revolutionary unions and to some extent in our unemployed councils is for these organizations to confine their efforts among Negroes to the placing of general demands such as equal rights on the job, no discrimination against Negroes, etc., and the failure to concretize these demands on the basis of the concrete conditions of the Negro workers in the individual shops, factories and neighborhoods. The tendency to gloss over the specific demands of the Negroes in some instances takes the form of actual resistance to struggle for these demands. This deviation in many cases is cloaked by seemingly radical phrases about no difference between Negro and white workers.

Behind this underestimation of the struggle for the demands of the Negro masses lies a deep-seated social democratic concept which regards the struggles of the Negro toilers against Jim Crowism and special persecution not as a part of the general struggles of the working class against capitalism but as something separate and apart from that struggle, as a struggle which does not strengthen but rather detracts from the general class struggle.

This reflects the survival within our ranks of the old antirevolutionary and essentially white chauvinist theory of the Lovestone renegades, the theory of the Negroes as "reserves of capitalist reaction." Without a continuous and vigorous fight both ideologically and organizationally against these dangerous tendencies, it will be impossible to carry through the task of the Fourteenth Plenum and the Open Letter in the field of Negro work.

The open letter reemphasizes the importance of the Negro question as a question of "allies of the American proletariat" and declares that "the Party can stand at the head of the national Revolutionary struggle of the Negro Masses against American imperialism only if it energetically carries through the decisions of the Fourteenth Plenum of the E[xecutive] C[ommittee] on the work among Negroes."

The main immediate task before the Party is the more energetic organization of the proletarian and semi-proletarian Negro masses into the Party and revolutionary mass organizations, particularly the revolutionary trade unions as an essential part of the carrying through of the policy of concentration. This task at the present time assumes tremendous importance from the standpoint of strengthening the hegemony of the working class and the leadership of the Party in the growing Negro national liberation struggles. The key to the successful carrying through of this task at the present moment lies in the energetic demands of the Negroes in connection with the Roosevelt National Recovery Act. The [National Industrial Recovery Administration] together with the Farm Relief Bill sharpens and legalizes the discrimination of Negro workers on the job and the robbery of the Negro poor farmers and sharecroppers on the plantations of the South. It means an all-around sharpening of the national oppression of the Negro people as witnessed in the new wave of lynchings in the South—Tuscaloosa, Decatur, and Selma, Alabama. The struggle against this increased oppression of the Negro masses must become an integral part of the whole campaign against the NIRA.

In all mass actions, strikes and unemployed struggles the Party must pay particular attention in the formulating practical expression to the special forms of exploitations, oppression and denial of the rights of the employed and unemployed Negro masses. (Open Letter.)

The emphasis upon the development of economic struggles among the Negro toilers does not mean to slacken but on the contrary to increase in every way the struggle around the general issues of Negro liberation, such as Scottsboro and the fight against lynching. It is necessary to broaden out and deepen these struggles, bringing forward our full program of social equality and right of self-determination and building up the broadest united front on these issues. Our chief task, however, is to bring this struggle into the shops and factories and on the land, linking it up with the more immediate demands of the Negro toilers, making the factories the main base in the struggle for Negro liberation and our trade unions the main lever for the organization of the Negro working class. At the same time the revolutionary mass organizations and particularly the trade unions must come forward more energetically in the struggle on behalf of the political demands of the Negro toilers.

This must go hand in hand with the ruthless combating of all forms of chauvinist and Jim Crow practices and the patient, systematic but persistent struggle against the ideology and influence of petty-bourgeois nationalists among the Negro toilers.

Only on this basis will the Party be able to give leadership to the rapidly developing upsurge of the Negro masses and to build this movement into a powerful weapon of the revolutionary proletariat for the weakening and destruction of the rule of American imperialism.

James W. Ford

*During the 1930s and the years of World War II, James W. Ford
(1893–1957) emerged from the CPUSA's Harlem section as one of the
most prominent black Communists in North America. Historians often
refer to Ford as symbolizing the party's attempt to construct a united front
between African Americans and the white working class. This young
black Communist also played the role of the champion of orthodoxy.*

*Ford ran for vice-president on the Communist Party ticket an un-
precedented three times, in 1932, 1936, and 1940. He was the first
African American to run on a presidential ticket in American history.
Ford served in the segregated U.S. Armed Forces during World War I.
After the war, he was a union militant in the American Postal Workers
Union. In 1925, he stepped forward as an activist in the American
Negro Labor Congress, a mass organization of black workers founded
and led by the CPUSA.*

*In the mid-1920s, Ford joined the American Communist Party
and quickly rose through the ranks as a promising young black leader.
In fact, he was sent to the Soviet Union as an American representative to
the Fourth World Congress of the Red International of Labor Unions.
Likewise, Ford took part in the Sixth World Congress of the Communist
International in 1928 and served on the Comintern's Negro Commis-
sion. Continuing his international activity as an African American
Communist, he also attended the Second Congress of the League against*

Imperialism. In 1929, he was chosen to head the International Trade Union Committee of Negro Workers and a year later became head of the Negro Department of the Trade Union Unity League.

Ford, in 1930, aided in the organization of the Comintern-sponsored First International Conference of Negro Workers. In 1932, he returned to the United States and was appointed to numerous leadership posts within the American Communist movement. For example, during the 1930s he accepted the post of vice-president of the League of Struggle for Negro Rights and as a representative on the Political Bureau of the CPUSA.

In 1933, as CPUSA placed increased emphasis on promoting black leaders, Ford was put in charge of the party's work in Harlem. In 1935, Ford was sent to the Seventh World Congress of the Communist International, then, as fascism was on the rise, he went to Spain to support the Republican forces in the Spanish Civil War. During the late 1930s, Ford was instrumental in founding the National Negro Congress. After World War II, the dissolution of the CPUSA by Earl Browder, and the party's re-founding, Ford continued to play an active role in the Communist Party, African American rights, peace, and socialism. He died in 1957.

▪ ▪ ▪

Pamphlets from the Reference Center for Marxist Studies Library, Tamiment Library and Robert F. Wagner Labor Archives, New York University

The Communists and the Struggle for Negro Liberation: Their Position on Problems of Africa, of the West Indies, of War, of Ethiopian Independence, of the Struggle of Peace

For the Emancipation of Negroes from Imperialism

Report to the Second World Congress of the League against Imperialism at Frankfurt, Germany, in July 1929. [Abridged]

1. General Statement

The so-called Negro "problem" has seldom been stated from the class point of view. We are in the period of the decline and decay of capitalism. Capitalism and imperialism are undergoing rapid change because of this decline. Everywhere the standards of living of the workers and peasants are being pushed down. Millions of workers throughout the world are thrown out of employment by the capitalist system. In the shops and factories and on the farms, workers and poor farmers are being forced to work at an increased speed. This is done in order that the capitalist may make greater profits at the expense of the workers.

This period of the decline of capitalism is of great significance to the working class and oppressed people, and is of very great importance to the Negro people in the various parts of the world. The future history of the Negro in his struggle for liberation, for political, social and economic advancement, depends upon how we estimate the present period of imperialism, the concrete organizational tasks that we lay down in order to bring about this liberation. We must mobilize our forces for joint struggle with the world proletariat in the international struggle against imperialism. We have already seen the great struggles of the Chinese workers and peasants. We see rising waves of revolt and struggle in India, and in China. We are witnessing great waves of revolt of the working class in the homelands of imperialism.

Imperialism and the Negro

For our purpose, in dealing with the special question of the Negro, imperialism is the stage of capitalism when the whole world has been divided among a few great capitalist powers, and especially when the territory of Africa has been completely divided between them; and when there has developed among the Negroes of America sharp class lines.

The World War Awakens Negroes

During the imperialist war of 1914–18 hundreds of thousands of Negroes from all parts of the world were brought into direct contact with the customs and "culture" of the so-called white western civilization. Millions of Negroes were brought from the agricultural and peasant regions of the Southern part of the U.S.A. into the industries of the North. This developed a huge Negro industrial proletariat. At the same time capitalism has carried industrial development into Africa, and there produced—especially in South Africa—a big native proletariat.

Already the period since the world war has brought about class-consciousness, revolt and resistance of Negro toilers against imperialism. But in order to understand the present period of the Negro's struggle, it is necessary for us to review briefly the older periods of exploitation and oppression of Negroes by the capitalists.

Policy of Imperialism

The economic and political enslavement of the Negro peoples has extended over a period of 300 years, and may be divided into three stages.

1. **The Classical Period**—the period of merchant capitalism, which was the period of snatching of slaves from Africa, marked the birth of the notorious African slave trade. This was the time when the Portuguese, the Dutch and the British capitalists were at the high tide of their business of stealing slaves from Africa. It has been said that over 100,000,000 Negroes were torn from Africa during the course of these 300 years. Great fortunes were made on the slave traffic.

Profits ranged from 100 per cent to 150 per cent on the sale of slaves. The average price of slaves was: in 1840, $325; in 1850, $360; in 1860, $500. It was on the basis of slave traffic profits, including the rape of India, that England was able to lay the basis of the British Empire. Also, great fortunes were made by the slave dealers in America. Thus it is clearly seen that capitalist exploitation for profits was the basis for the beginning of the enslavement of the Negro people.

2. **The Second Period**—the period of industrial capitalism—was the beginning of the territorial division of Africa, and the exploitation of its natural resources, and the labor power of the natives in Africa. Because the slave traffic became less profitable for the capitalists, this period marked the beginning of the doing away with the "legal" slave traffic. It was during this period that the natural resources of Africa helped to build up the great manufacturing enterprises in England. In America the doing away with the slave traffic was replaced by the intense plantation exploitation of the Negro

slaves. The profits made on the plantation exploitation of the Negro slave laid the basis for the present wealth of American imperialism. Thus the stopping of the slave traffic did not stop the profit making of the capitalists. It merely increased their profit making.

3. **The Third Stage**—and this is the period that we are most concerned with—is the period of imperialism. This period marks the completion of the division of Africa by the main capitalist powers, and marks the complete enslavement of its people. This period also is the period when the main capitalist powers are organizing to fight each other for the redivision of Africa. It is a period also when the workers are being speeded up and exploited at a greater rate by the capitalists in order to make more profits. Hundreds of thousands and millions of Negro toilers are being thrown out of work. But at the same time the Negro toilers everywhere are struggling against this extreme exploitation and oppression. Widespread revolt is spreading among Negro toilers in different parts of the world.

The Modern Policy of Imperialism

What is the policy of imperialism? Imperialism is holding the African colonies as "country sides" for agricultural development. All the imperialists are hindering the industrial development of the country to this end. They are therefore carrying on a policy which perpetually hinders the advancement of the toiling masses. They actually exterminate the people by the thousands, killing the populations and destroying whole towns.

Africa is a leading source of raw materials, a market center for extra capital investment. The markets and raw materials are becoming short. This is the main reason for the jealousy and rivalry between the various capitalist countries and is leading them to war.

The Native Workers of South Africa

The great majority of the South African population is Negro. There are about five and one-half millions of native Negroes and colored, and about one and one-half millions of whites. The Negroes are the majority of the working class. There are 467,013 or about 70 per cent Negro and colored workers, and about 176,073 or 23 per cent white workers. In mining there are over 300,000 Negroes to about 40,000 whites. In transportation there are 40,000 Negroes and

66,000 whites; in the general production industries there are 20,000 Negroes and 71,000 whites.

In the Belgian Congo in 1919 in the gold, copper and diamond mines there were 31,000 native workers; in 1926 there were 61,000; in the Union of Katagu there, were 16,448 native workers.

Agricultural Workers

In South Africa the native and colored population may be divided as follows:

(1) Natives on their own tribal lands (reserves) 51%
(2) Natives on European-owned lands 34%
(3) Native workers in mines and cities 14%

The agricultural output has gradually increased in South Africa. The export in 1910 was 9,500,000 pounds; in 1927 it was 22,000,000 pounds. The number of dairy factories increased from 59 to 124 during the period of 1915–25.

In Sierra Leone, Nigeria and the whole West Coast of Africa there are vast agricultural developments. The same is true of the Belgian Congo.

In South Africa the native reserves form only one-eighth of the total land of the Union, and natives are not allowed to buy land outside of the reserves. Certain lands that were to be turned back to the natives are being given to the white settlers, for example, large sections suitable for cotton growing in Northern Transvaal. The existing reserves are totally insufficient for the natives. A large number of natives are compelled for this reason and also because of taxation and the pressure of the native chiefs (who act as agents for the government) to go out and work in the white lands. One-third of the native adult male population is all the time away at work in the towns or on the farms.

West Indies

The West Indies are typically agricultural islands. The West Indian Islands are under the iron hand of the imperialists. Haiti is under the iron heel of the American marines of the National City Bank of Wall Street. The independence of Haiti gained during the Haitian revolution when French domination was overthrown has been completely nullified by the U.S. marines. The people have been garroted, and are being ruled by the American imperialists. The country, in spite of its natural richness, is in poverty, the like of which has not been seen since the days before the Haitian revolution.

In Trinidad the natives are ruled by the iron hand of British imperialism. The workers are suppressed by the troops of the British Empire stationed there.

In Guadeloupe the same thing is true. Here French imperialism keeps the workers and peasants down to the level of slaves.

Here we find some kind of "community" improvement resorted to: Natives at the points of bayonets of U.S. marines (Haiti) are forced to build roads without pay. Negroes in Haiti and Jamaica are conscripted for work on the sugar plantations of Cuba. They are taken to Cuba and forced in work for wages lower than the Cuban workers, and racial frictions are engendered between the imported natives and the workers of Cuba.

Tactics in the Struggle Against Imperialism

The struggle for liberation is found only through organization, organization along class lines, for class struggle. Our struggle is bound up with the struggle of the international proletariat and we must line up in the international revolutionary class struggle the world over, by organizing our forces for joint struggle. It is necessary to follow a trade union program. This program must be based on the following demands:

Equal pay for equal work.
An Eight-Hour Day.
Against forced labor.
For protective labor legislation.
Protection for women and youth workers.
Freedom of trade unions.
Against class cooperation.
Against racial barriers in trade unions.
Organization of Negro workers into revolutionary trade
    unions.
Against white terrorism and lynchings.

Organization of defense corps.

Better housing and social conditions.

Organization of agricultural workers.

Against the confiscation of peasant and communal lands.

Against poll tax and hut tax.

For equal civil rights.

Liberation Movements

The liberation movements of Negro peoples take different forms in different countries. The main thing is that they must be initiated by the toiling masses of workers and peasants. The demands of the great bulk of the population must be the center of action. No liberation movement of the Negroes can be helpful for the Negro masses unless the masses are driving force. Liberation movements cannot play a decisive role in the liberation of the Negroes representing partial middle class demands of the petty-bourgeoisie and intellectuals. If the petty-bourgeoisie and the intellectuals want to serve the masses they must be the servants of the masses, and the masses must see that they are their servants.

The program of liberation movements must also offer the masses real assistance in their desperate need and conditions. For this it is necessary to have a program. . . .

Pamphlets from the Reference Center for Marxist Studies Library, Tamiment Library and Robert F. Wagner Labor Archives, New York University

The Communists and the Struggle for Negro Liberation: Their Position on Problems of Africa, of the West Indies, of War, of Ethiopian Independence, of the Struggle of Peace

Introduction

Can Garveyism and Communism Mix?

This question as answered by some of the leading members of the Universal Negro Improvement Association can only breed disunity among the Negro masses at a time when united organization and action is imperative. Of course, there are many points in the programs of the two movements which differ. But both are agreed that black men should be freed from the domination of imperialists in Africa and throughout the world. We both agree that Mussolini's fascist hordes should be driven from Ethiopia; that Ethiopia's independence must be maintained. However different our ultimate aims for society as a whole we are agreed on all points against imperialism, whether in Africa, West Indies, or America, such as Africa for Africans, self-determination for Africa and the West Indies, the independence of Ethiopia.

Those who argue against unity of action NOW are in the position of the man who would not accept the help of his friend in moving the furniture from his burning house because the friend wanted to advise WHERE the furniture should go LATER. Well, let us unite to save Ethiopia and safeguard the black man's rights NOW. History will determine as to who is right about what is to be done later.

It is no idle reflection that if the Negroes had been really united and had known how to effect and utilize allies among other nationalities, Ethiopia today would be a jar different story.

Who Are Mussolini's Enemies?

Some of the leaders still cry "Stop Communism!" "Expel the Reds!" Those who do this are consciously or unconsciously aiding the followers and supporters of Mussolini. For it is well known that Mussolini so fears the Communists among his own people that thousands of them now grace his dungeons. Shall we join with Mussolini to crush the Communists or join with the Communists to crush Mussolini? Negroes certainly cannot ignore the old military axiom: "Seek out your enemy's enemy for an ally."

It is, therefore, a question of which whites can be considered allies of the Negro organizations, which whites will support the program aimed at world freedom for the blacks. Let us see!

[William Randolph] Hearst and the Republicans have already shown their alliance with Mussolini. They are carrying on powerful propaganda each day for recognition of his steal. This is coupled with their activities in this country promoting the Ku Klux Klan organizations, fighting labor organizations, and belittling Negroes generally. If [Fiorello] La Guardia represents fusion, his activities in raising money for the fascist Red Cross is a good indication of where this white group stands. Besides this, the Mayor has a medal of honor from Mussolini himself, and has nothing but praise for the Italian Government.

The Democrats who control the government have said nothing about the rape of Ethiopia and will not even aid those other powers on a world scale to enforce the decisions of the League of Nations. Judges Cotillo, Aurelio, and Pecora, Tammanyites, are open supporters of Mussolini in this country, cooperating with the fascist consuls throughout the country, in whipping up pro-Mussolini sentiment among the Italian masses.

Police Attack Ethiopian Defense

These are the most outstanding cases. But what about DeMartini, the police inspector in Harlem and his Negro stooges, who try to stop the protest of Harlem Negroes against the conquest of Ethiopia? Who is responsible for the oversized police "army of occupation" in Harlem following the fall of Addis Ababa?

Who is responsible for allowing Italian Consuls to carry on fascist propaganda in America, despite diplomatic agreements with the United States Government?

Yet there are some members of the U.N.I.A. who would unite the organization with the political programs of one or the other of the above-mentioned groups. In other words, they would use the "red scare" to win support among Negroes for those whites who have everything in their power to defeat the cause of Negro freedom have done everything in their power to defeat the cause of Negro freedom here and help consolidate Mussolini's ill-gotten gains in Ethiopia.

United Action Can Defeat the Fascist Invasion

We should unite to demand that the fascist consuls be restrained from propaganda work in this country! Demand the removal and censure of pro-fascist American officials.

Demand action from the State Department against Italian conquest in Ethiopia; aid in enforcing economic sanctions; no recognition of the fascist mandate!

Demand Harlem representatives in city, state, and national bodies present resolutions favoring Ethiopian independence!

Organize perpetual picketing of Italian consulates with the Ethiopian flag by a united Ethiopian Defense.

Boycott Italian imports and arouse Negro and white longshore workers against military shipments to Italy.

Only a united mass defense can yet save a bleeding Ethiopia from the clutches of the fascist brute.

Mr. Garvey has shown the way by co-operating with the anti-imperialist league in England. Let us follow by building a powerful movement here for defense of Ethiopia and the rights of Black men everywhere.

Disunity and wrangling means demoralization and defeat; the united front leads to victory and regeneration.

For these things we Communists have always, do, and always will stand ready.

Harlem Division of the Communist Party.

Pamphlets from the Reference Center for Marxist Studies Library, Tamiment Library and Robert F. Wagner Labor Archives, New York University

Ethiopia

An Interview with Minister Tecle Hawariate, Ethiopian Delegate at Geneva, Sees Aid of Negroes as "FAR-REACHING, POTENT AND POWERFUL"

Coincident with the opening of the dramatic sixteenth session of the League of Nations at Geneva, Switzerland, on September 9th, where the Ethiopian Delegation began a political and diplomatic struggle in defense of the independence of its country, a conference of far-reaching significance was held between an American delegation and the Ethiopian representatives.

The conference was held with the Ethiopian Ambassador and Minister Plenipotentiary, *Bedjironde Tecle Hawariate,* and Charge D'Affaires of the Paris Legation of Ethiopian, *Ephrem Tewolde*

Medhen. The Ethiopian representatives received the American delegation with the utmost cordiality and hospitality.

They left the morning sessions of the League and met with the delegation at their hotel, Hotel De Russe. Although in the midst of the busiest and perhaps most important diplomatic session of the League of Nations since the World War, the Ethiopian Ambassador let it be known that the conference was of such importance that he would give whatever time necessary to send a message to the American people.

The American Delegation consisted of William N. Jones, staff correspondent of the Baltimore *Afro-American,* James W. Ford, Communist leader, representing the Provisional Committee for the Defense of Ethiopia and who was on his way to meet with a group of well-known liberals in Paris in connection with a world movement for the defense of Ethiopia, and Benjamin Careathers of the League of Struggle for Negro Rights, of Pittsburgh, Pa.

U.S. Delegation Reports on Ethiopian Defense

Following formal introduction, Mr. William N. Jones opened the conference by presenting a prepared list of questions and introducing James W. Ford, who outlined the aims of the visit of the American Delegation and the protest actions which had already been carried through in the United States and other parts of the world, particularly the actions of the Negroes in Harlem, Chicago, Cleveland and other parts of the U.S.A. He told of the splendid support which had been given by the Negro press in the U.S.A. He also told of sympathetic actions in behalf of Ethiopia, which were taking place among. Negro people in South Africa, Paris, London, West Indies, etc. . . .

What Is the World Going to Do?

"The world has passed its sentiment morally, but it remains to be seen whether it is to be put into practice," he said. "In Africa there are only left Liberia and Ethiopia. The only specimen of an independent country remaining is Ethiopia; it remains expressive of the right of colored nations to independence."

At this tense and dramatic moment (and everyone in that room was tense and filled with emotion) Mr. Hawariate said emphatically:

"*That is the question!* All People must see the outcome of this question as the rights of all human beings, or, is it to be limited by the color of one's skin!"

Then Mr. Hawariate said calmly and deliberately: "I understand your sympathies from both viewpoints. Our sympathies are naturally spontaneous. But let alone you're your sentiments, some who are alien (in race) feel for us."

Compliments Our Activities in U.S.A.

[Hawariate continued,] "Your activities in the United States in our behalf are highly appreciated and I want to thank the American people not only for myself but for my people. I feel that it has been useful, beneficial and *powerful!*"

"There are many factors," he said, "and we expect great sacrifices, but we have full faith in the outcome. This solidarity in the U.S.A. assures me of our final success."

What More Can Be Done?

Considerable time was taken by Mr. Hawariate in discussion of practical methods of support to Ethiopia. He said: "You must now carefully study future methods to be undertaken to help Ethiopia. We have had offers from all colors—white, brown, yellow and black.

"But what Ethiopia lacks is not men, we have sufficient for fighting purposes. In this regard we have never yet acceded in any way to Italy. What is really our problem? Ethiopia needs war materials and munitions, and medical and flying assistance is useful. If we are in need of finance it is only for that purpose, and no other. We are limited in the money required for that purpose, compared to Italy. We are handicapped in the sense that Italy has unlimited access to war materials as she wishes.

"It is a question of armaments: here finance plays the whole role. The greatest help or contribution which American Negroes can render is on the financial side. There is not one American Negro that would not give his last penny for Ethiopia's cause. His motive for so doing is because he feels that Ethiopia symbolizes independence and national life. His benefit is not of a material but of an idealistic nature: to show that colored people are just as much human beings as white people."

Warns Against Profiteers and Self-Seekers

This question of finances, however, Mr. Hawariate stated, is one which should be handled with extreme care and caution.

"There is something which I am afraid of," he said, "if American Negroes contribute money *it should go for what it is intended*—to save the independence and nation of Ethiopia, and for no other purpose. But as you know, in the ordinary run of life such things look simple yet in the carrying out of them difficulties are encountered not only of a purely technical character, but in the handling of money, of a speculative kind.

"Therefore I want to warn that if the American Negro population gives, you must never forget that there are profiteers and speculators. It must be seen to that the money is utilized to help those intended. If this practical point is kept in mind, the plan will be beneficial. If the money, however, goes into the hands of speculators there will be regret on both sides." With those suggestions, Mr. Hawariate closed his remarks.

Mr. William N. Jones then put several questions to Mr. Hawariate.

Question: "Has the Ethiopian government, or any group with authority to do so, made connection with any group in the U.S.A. to raise funds for Ethiopian defense?"

Answer: Mr. Hawariate replied that to his knowledge, "No! My proposals are personal suggestions."

Question: "What is the attitude of the Ethiopian government to the recent declaration of Mussolini that nothing would satisfy him except domination of Ethiopia?"

Answer: "Ethiopia is a member of the League of Nations," he replied, "signatory to the League Covenant, which has been signed by every nation affiliated to the League. We only ask that this pact be put to work. But if the League proves itself powerless, we are prepared to defend ourselves. The Ethiopians have the same desire for independence other people have, and they also have the will to fight for it."

Praises Litvinoff

Question: "What do you have to say to the support given Ethiopia by the Soviet representative? You should be informed that certain people in the U.S.A. claim that Mr. Litvinoff (at the time that he was presiding as chairman of the League Council at a previous session) and the Soviet government betray the interest of Ethiopia and that of colored people in general."

Answer: (Interjection by Mr. Medhen, Ethiopian Charge D'Affaires: "They are mistaken.") "I think that he (Litvinoff) spoke and acted right; not only Mr. Litvinoff but other representatives, such as those of Denmark, Argentina and Spain have openly expressed their favorable stand. Mr. Litvinoff did not offend Ethiopia. What he speaks and does is sincere. I find him genuine!"

Question: "Is not the national interest of small nation like Czecho-Slovakia involved in the Ethiopian situation to such an extent that it is to the interest of all small nations to stand solidly behind Ethiopia?"

Answer: "The fact that Czecho-Slovakia and certain Balkan states sympathize with us (and others have expressed their support privately) shows that they feel themselves and their national independence involved."

Pamphlets from the Reference Center for Marxist Studies Library,
Tamiment Library and Robert F. Wagner Labor Archives,
New York University

Communists in the Fight for Negro Rights

"HAVE Communists quit fighting for Negro rights?"

This is indeed a strange question to ask me and my colleagues, Benjamin J. Davis, Jr., New York City Councilman, and William L. Patterson, Assistant Director of the Lincoln School in Chicago. Despite the perverted form of the question it establishes a fact of great historical significance in the life of the Negro people and the democratic life of the nation—the fact that the Communists have played a particularly outstanding role in the destiny of our people.

It is no accident that attention is focused particularly on the Communists in the struggle for Negro rights. For, in the last twenty-five years, it has been the Communists who have not only been in advance of all sections of the population in this struggle, but for a long time were pretty much alone in it, and the Negro people have acquired a profound appreciation of the struggle of the Communists for Negro rights.

Why have the Communists been consistently fighting for Negro rights? It is because they are opposed to oppression of any people; because they have always understood that labor in the white skin cannot be free, nor can democracy be secure, as long as the Negro people are enthralled; because they know that the disfranchisement of the Negro is one of the pillars of reaction in the country, directed also against the people and every progressive current. American democracy could not be healthy if it rested upon the oppression of a tenth of the population.

This approach is part of the fundamental conception of the Communist movement and allows of no compromise, and the record of the Communists demonstrates to the satisfaction of the Negro people that at no time have the Communists compromised on this question, so basic for the American labor movement and for the progressive development of the country.

It is not my intention to review this record. I will take only the example which provides the most decisive test of all, namely the Communist position on the Negro question in our present war of national survival. This is a war against fascism, and every honest and sincere opponent of reaction and oppression in any form understood immediately that only the complete defeat and destruction of fascism in this war could assure continuation of human progress, and that all other considerations would have to be subordinated to this central objective. This is the way the Negro people as a whole have approached it. On this both are in full accord.

Those who insinuate that the Communists have given up the struggle for Negro rights really want to say two things: (a) that victory in the war and the fight for Negro rights have nothing to do with one another; (b) that the Communists place victory in the war above the defense of Negro rights.

This confusion, to put it mildly, is of no service to our country and of still less service to the Negro people. On the first point, no thoughtful and sincere spokesman for the Negro people will claim victory in the war against Negro rights. He understands that the two are inseparable, for the simple reason that victory for fascism would not only rob the American nation of its independence and democratic gains but would mean the greatest disaster particularly for the Negro people.

The real question has been how to strengthen our war effort by securing equal rights for the Negro people and that is how the Communists have placed this question. Earl Browder has repeatedly declared in behalf of the Communist movement:

"The Jim-Crow system is the outgrowth of the ideology of 'white supremacy' which is just as shameful and dangerous for America as Hitler's identical racialism proved to be for Germany and the world. . . . JIM CROW MUST GO IF AMERICA IS TO STAND."

Is this what is called "stopping" the fight for Negro rights?

Had the Negro people followed the counsel of disregarding their stake in the war it would not only have weakened national unity against fascism but would have undermined the historic and undeniable advances of the Negro people during the war.

Had they followed this policy they would have betrayed the American labor movement which as a result of the efforts of the Communists has emerged as the strongest champion of Negro rights. Labor rightly regards this war against fascism as its own most sacred war. Surely to ask the Negro people to let down their labor allies raises the question of the soundness of this whole policy; and the best proof of the correctness of the Negro people joining with white labor in national unity behind the war, is the leading role which labor had played during this war in fighting for and securing Negro rights.

What is involved here is not the question of the Communists "stopping" the fight for Negro rights but the whole question of what is the best path for the Negro people. The Communists raised the Negro question as a national question and a question of democracy and proceeded to organize the struggle for equal rights. In this war it received its greatest test.

As a result of this policy, first advanced by the Communists and the labor movement, the Negro people are one of the strongest sources of democratic strength in the country, successfully integrating themselves into the nation.

The alternative would have been helping fascism to victory by depriving our national unity of one of its important pillars—support of the Negro people—and depriving the Negro people of their most important ally—the white labor movement—and hampering the one administration, under President Roosevelt's leadership, which has done more for Negro rights than any other administration since Lincoln's day.

Benjamin J. Davis Jr.

Harlem citizens elected Benjamin J. Davis Jr. (1903–1964), African American attorney and Communist, to the New York City Council in 1943. Not surprisingly, as the Cold War heated up in post–World War II America, Davis endured increasing hostility from beyond New York. Indeed, in 1951 federal authorities convicted Davis, along with ten other national CPUSA leaders, of violating the Smith Act and sentenced him to five years in federal prison.

As young man, Davis proved to be academically gifted and ambitious. Born and raised in Dawson, Georgia, he successfully completed Morehouse College's high school program in Atlanta. Afterward, he pursued higher education at Amherst College, where he obtained his bachelor of arts degree. Subsequently, in 1930, he graduated from Harvard Law School and worked briefly as a journalist before starting a law practice in Atlanta.

During the early 1930s, Davis represented Angelo Herndon, a nineteen-year-old African American communist charged with violating Georgia's law against "attempting to incite insurrection." In fact, Herndon had been organizing a farmworkers' union. Throughout the trial, Davis encountered discriminatory hostility from the judge and the white community. He was also deeply impressed by the rhetoric and courage of Herndon and his Leftist colleagues. As the trial ended, he joined the Communist Party. Convicted and sentenced to eighteen to twenty years in prison, Herndon was soon freed when the courts ruled that Georgia's insurrection law was unconstitutional.

Davis left the South in 1,935 and moved to Harlem, where he worked as the editor of the Negro Liberator *and, later, of the Communist Party's newspaper, the* Daily Worker. *In 1943, he was elected to fill a City Council seat vacated by Adam Clayton Powell Jr., who had left to run for the U.S. Congress. Voters twice reelected Davis to his City Council seat. However, in 1949 he was expelled from the council after his Smith Act conviction. His removal from office was required under state law. Furthermore, he appealed the conviction without success over a two-year period. Subsequently, after three years and four months in the federal penitentiary in Terre Haute, Indiana, authorities freed Davis.*

In the years after his release, Davis spoke on several major college campuses and remained politically active by promoting an agenda of civil rights and economic populism. In 1962, he spoke at Harvard, Columbia, Amherst, Oberlin, and the University of Minnesota. Nonetheless, as an ironic twist in his political biography, the City College of New York (in the New York Council District he represented in the 1940s) barred Davis from speaking on its campus. After a number of student protests, however, Davis was permitted to speak on a nearby street.

In the early 1960s, federal authorities charged Davis with violating the Internal Security Act. He died before the case went to trial. Davis was running for the New York State Senate on the People's Party ticket when he died from lung cancer in 1964.

▪ ▪ ▪

Special Collections: University Archives Manuscript Collection, MS 102, Box 28, State University of New York, Buffalo

Reply to a Loaded Question

Pamphlet: "Communists in the Struggle for Negro Rights," in *Communists in the Struggle for Negro Rights,* by James W. Ford, Benjamin J. Davis Jr., William L. Patterson, and Earl Browder (New York: New Century Publishers, 1945).

"Have Communists quit fighting for Negro rights?"—is, of course, a loaded question. Apparently, certain gentlemen on the affirmative are, at least, willing to confess that the Communists once did fight for Negro rights; and, I understand, honest confession is good for the soul. Communists have struggled along for Negro rights under the tremendous handicap of being without the eminent acknowledgement by these gentlemen of what we were doing, and have pulled through as best as they could. But we were nevertheless happy to see a past truth conceded about the Communists, even if it is done for the purpose of denying a present truth about the Communists.

The real question that certain of these gentlemen on the affirmative would like to discuss is the Communists' position in support of the war. For them the query, "Have Communists quit fighting for Negro rights?" is a smoke screen to conceal their own internal, unresolved conflict on how they stand on the war. Communists are unequivocal on this question. They regard this war as what it is— just and a patriotic people's war of national liberation, to rid the world of fascism and all its works, and to build a durable peace of security, freedom and prosperity for all mankind. Communists are proud of their self-sacrificing support of our country and the United Nations in this war and join with all Americans—black and white—in placing victory in the war and in peace above all else.

The greatest service that can be contributed to Negro rights is unconditional support of the war, without which equality and freedom is impossible for any people. Anyone who is equivocal on this supreme task cannot help and is not helping the cause of Negro rights—he is helping Hitler and world fascism.

The abolition of Jim Crow, anti-Semitism and all other forms of racial discrimination on the home front is a part of this worldwide struggle. The Communists were the first to insist that precisely because we were engaged in a struggle against world fascism, our country must cleanse itself of all "white supremacy" practices at home now. Said Earl Browder, now President of the Communists Political Association, in 1942: "These issues (fight against Jim Crow—B.D.) cannot be evaded or glossed over. It is not a contribution to national unity to be silent about them. This is not something that can be postponed in the interests of national unity for victory, for this is of the very essence of democracy and the remedy of these profound abuses a precondition for victory." Again, in his book, *Teheran—Our Path in War and Peace,* published in 1944, Browder said: "Jim Crow must go if America is to stand." This, of course, is not an isolated percept, but constitutes a guide to action for all Communists.

Like Frederick Douglass, who supported Lincoln in the Civil War against chattel slavery and simultaneously fought against Jim Crow bars in the Union armies; the Communists today support President Roosevelt in the war against fascist slavery and simultaneously fight against these practices at home. Communists are resolutely fighting for the elimination of Scottsboro frame-ups in and out of the armed forces; for strong unions based upon the principle of equality of membership and equality of pay; for decent facilities for underprivileged Negro communities; and for the immediate, unconditional citizenship of Negro Americans in all walks of life.

When, in 1943, to pardon a personal reference, both major parties failed to guarantee the election of a Negro to the City Council in New York, the Communists stepped into the breach, put forward a candidate on a non-partisan bias, and thus saved the biggest city in the world from the shame of no Negro legislative representation in the midst of a war for national liberation.

Conscious of the new and higher forms of struggle necessitated by the civil war crisis of our country, it is obvious that Communists have resolutely upheld the banner for the abolition of the Jim-Crow system. These facts are well-known among informed people; and it is futile to detail them at length to professional anti-Communists who make a living by vilifying and misrepresenting the Communists in order to paralyze, confuse and divide the people.

Such Red-baiters as the fifth column Trotskyites and the Norman Thomas "socialists," are the principal agitators of the query, "Have Communists quit fighting for Negro rights?" Their concern, however, is not for the Negroes; nor are they out to save the Communists from themselves. It is their purpose to sharpen their traitorous opposition to the nation, but very helpful to Hitler. If a straightforward and not a loaded question is desired: When is this motley crew going to stop doing Hitler's dirty work in our country?

Chapter 13: Life in the Terre Haute Penitentiary

Ben Davis, *Communist Councilman from Harlem: Autobiographical Notes Written in a Federal Penitentiary* [First Edition] (New York: International Publishers, 1969).

I arrived at the Terre Haute penitentiary July 10, 1951. (That the city of Terre Haute, birthplace of Eugene V. Debs, should be the site of a dungeon for working-class champions is enough to make the great socialist leader turn over in his grave.) On July 6, six of us—Dennis, Gates, Williamson, Winter, Potash and I—had been transported on the prison bus from the Federal Detention House on West Street to Lewisburg Penitentiary in Pennsylvania. The seventh prisoner, Stachel, remained in New York to be routed directly to the Danbury, Conn., federal penitentiary. At Lewisburg, we were divided and routed as follows: Dennis and Gates to Atlanta; Winter and Williamson to Lewisburg; Potash to Leavenworth; and I to Terre Haute. In October 1951, Gus Hall was kidnapped from Mexico in gangster fashion by the FBI and later sent to Leavenworth.

Because of his heart ailment, Stachel was sent to Danbury, supposedly one of the "easiest" prisons. (I shall never forget Prosecutor McGohey's reply to a humane and reasonable request for the continuance of Stachel's bail: "Oh, indeed, your honor, prison is good for heart ailments.")

As can be seen, the government took pains to divide us, allowing no more than two of the leaders in the same penitentiary. It is anybody's guess why, but it added to our punishment, denying us companionship and making the going that much harder for those who were alone. It denied us the opportunity to pool our mutual knowledge and interests. The government perhaps feared our being together and even in jail, encircled by umpteen officers and steel bars every foot or so. But this hardly explains the special honor extended to me. I was stuck off by myself in a state notorious for its Ku Klux Klan and so close to the site of the Cicero, Illinois, white-supremacy outbreak; I could almost feel it down my neck. Since I was the only Negro among the jailed Communist leaders, a terrific problem confronted the champions of democracy who run government. To have put me together with a white leader would have placed too great a strain upon the system of segregation prevailing in the federal prison system. The friendship which would have been demonstrated between me and one of my fellow-Communists would have been a bad example for the other Negro and white prisoners.

Actually this was my first time in jail—except for a hot moment for union picketing and the three-week stretch in West Street. In prisoner's parlance, a five-year sentence is not regarded as exactly beginner's luck. By and large, I have been treated like all the other Negros prisoners. The occasional exceptions did not mean special favors—which I neither asked for nor received. Although I am without experience in this field, prison is prison and the life becomes almost insufferable at times. The atmosphere is oppressive and the prison routine enervating. Washington, in violation of even the prison rules, clamped extra restrictions upon my correspondence, allowing me at first to correspond with no one but my sister and my attorney. Inmates are normally permitted to have seven on their correspondents' list.

In prison, one is beset by mental frustration, emotional and spiritual starvation and by a benumbing prison routine enforced by the threat of violence in the prison's punitive measures. Both extremes are to be found—the bitterest curing and the most disgusting cringing—sometimes both in the same prisoner. There are all sorts of complex cross-currents which one does well to be aware of.

One learns soon to guard against three major hazards—deterioration of health, mental stagnation, and emotional unbalance. It is particularly depressing to become ill in prison. To prevent this, you can take exercise in the "recreation yard"—baseball, softball, basketball, football, calisthenics, weight-lifting, horseshoe pitching and other sports. In my zeal for exercise, soon after I arrived I sprained my ankle playing baseball. Then, as luck would have it, I had trouble with a displaced disc in my back and ended up in the prison hospital for three weeks. As a result, I had to sleep on a bed board in my cell—not that the bed was not hard enough to begin with. But the board made the concrete hardness uniform instead of bumpy. I finally compromised on a few regular calisthenics in my cell. This proved to be more in keeping with my age and was proof against the weather, since the prison had no gymnasium for indoor sports.

Mental stagnation is not only bad in itself, but it can easily undermine physical health. Either you become conscious of this and combat it, or else you sink to one of the lower levels of prison existence. One of the most virulent forms of deterioration is brooding and self-pity. This is bad enough for justices of the Supreme Court—not to mention millions of other Americans—had held to be wrongfully jailed, the temptation to brood is strong indeed. This injustice of being in jail while crooks, thieves, war makers, anti-Semites and lynchers roam the streets is a difficult fact of life to adjust to. I never did succeed in wholly accomplishing serenity. Worst of all, to be barred from participation in the struggle for peace—the supreme issue of this mid-century—and for the liberation of the Negro and the colonial peoples, was the greatest threat to equilibrium.

On the other hand, there is the danger of a state of mind which regards everything that happens in prison as being of supreme importance. You seek to keep face within the community—a custom that flows naturally out of the isolated, stratified chapter of prison society. The least thing can be upsetting; pretty soon the environment of pettiness can becomes one's whole world. One has to learn to pick and choose what is of value and to avoid the "inner politics" of prison life. I sought to concentrate my main interest on those matters that were directly concerned with the real problems of society.

And, of course, it is not only the body but the mind which is imprisoned. The books, newspapers and periodicals I wanted to read and study were at the head of the *verboten* list: Marx, Lenin, Stalin, Foster, and the *Daily Worker*. Even though I was in prison and could "conspire" with no one, I was still not permitted to read Communist books. Unable to jail the books themselves, the government went to the worse outrage of putting the readers of such books in jail. But the library was jam-packed with the scribbling of Communist slanderers. There were two or three copies of Hitler's *Mein Kampf.*

Nevertheless, I found a certain value in acquiring some useful knowledge and in reading neglected books. The library did contain many valuable volumes—many of a classical character—which were not only worth reading but afforded opportunity for study and reflection—history, natural science, biography. My assignment to the library, which included handling books and manicuring the floor, greatly facilitated systematic reading, and I took full advantage of it.

An interesting irony is that Prosecutor McGohey had said during the trial that my "weapons were books," and that I now found myself assigned to handle more "weapons" in Terre Haute.

I was struck by the fact that once a dialectical outlook has been acquired, then such subjects as economics, natural science, history, and above all mathematics (which may seem disconnected in bourgeois education), fall naturally into place. It will be a fine day for American kids when, under a socialist system, they learn that life is an integrated whole and that all studies are to enable man to be happier, to conquer life and nature.

Thus, reading became one of the most effective breaks in my prison routine. But I needed relief from that, too, if only to rest my eyes. For current literature, my friends on the outside sent me subscriptions to the *New York Times,* Time magazine and the *Pittsburgh Courier*—the largest of the Negro weeklies. This was the best my friends and I could do.

When I arrived at Terre Haute, the "velvet carpet," so to speak, had been prepared for me. Pictures of jailed Communist leaders adorned every front page, headlines blinded the eyes, and radio commentators assaulted the ears. Seven of the Communist national board members were at last under lock and key—the country could breathe easier, although prices kept right on going up, the wages kept going down, and the lynch system continued to claim its black victims. Whatever people thought of our socialist convictions, even the most naïve ought to have been able to see that we were not responsible for ills actually afflicting them.

What the inmates at Terre Haute, and perhaps even some of the administration, who had never seen a Communist in the flesh, expected me to be like, I cannot imagine. From the flamboyant notoriety, was I expected to breathe fire and brimstone from my nostrils? I'm sure there were fears that I would "agitate" for my political views, and an agitator is just about the last thing any prison wants. If the government's publicity had grossly misrepresented my views, quite a few of the prisoners felt that they, too, had been misrepresented by the courts and that they shouldn't be here—that much, at least, we had in common.

Quite a few of the inmates were aggressively anti-communist; sometimes from conviction; sometimes deliberately provocative. This hostility was manifested in jibes and sniping, and occasionally an attempt at missionary preaching to show me the error of my ways. Others went so far as to show me how lucky I was to be living in this great free country. And here we all were, in jail! A few of the inmates felt that they did not know enough about communism to be pro or con. Of course, I talked only to a comparative few; they could not resist the temptation to ask if what they read in the papers about me was true. And there was something in the paper almost daily.

In many instances, my sense of humor—which no one ever thought too much of—served me well. At some of the ridiculous jibes, I couldn't keep from laughing. They would seem more like slapstick comedy than serious questions. I could not undertake to answer all the innuendos and loaded questions. I did not have to be imprisoned to know that life of a communist in the U.S. was no bed of roses—being a Negro had left me no stranger to persecution.

Among the things I did to get away from the unpleasant facts of life in prison was my attempt to take one course at the prison school—Conversational Spanish, taught by one of the Latin American inmates. For a long time I had wanted to speak Spanish because of the large Spanish-speaking population in Harlem, with whom we Negroes had so much in common. I regretted that so few of our comrades had mastered the language. And I always envied William Foster who, though he had never had half as much formal education as I, spoke many languages and had a reading knowledge of still others. He always warned us about the tendency to think that only the citizens of the United States were Americans. His work, *Outline Political History of the Americas,* was a fundamental refutation of this kind of national chauvinism. He put great stock in the belief that it was part of the fight against chauvinist prejudices to learn the language of other people and converse with them in their own tongue. It's too bad I had to go to jail before I did much about it. (I'm sure the Department of Justice speculates that I'm taking Spanish so that I can escape abroad when I am released.)

If, as the federal system officials contend, the purpose of prison is to rehabilitate the prisoner, this is surely a long way from it. Just how was I to be rehabilitated? By being taught the virtues of capitalism, with the prison demonstrating such virtues so admirably? Can anyone with a straight face promulgate such virtues when capitalism is so bankrupt all over the world that Wall Street has to prop it up? It's capitalism that could do with a little rehabilitation—not I or my fellow Communist prisoners.

The fact that there is no special status for political prisoners in the United States is one more evidence of the backwardness of our social system. In Europe, even prior to [World War II], such a status existed in many capitalist European countries. If the more enlightened penologists were inclined to grant a more humane status to political prisoners, the McCarrans and Joe McCarthys and other flag-wavers would hound them out of public life.

Neither I nor any other Communist chooses to be a martyr. We fought with all the resources at our command to prevent this government from doing such violence to traditional American liberties, to save the American working people from "thought control" persecution and from the catastrophe of another world war. That fight will go on no matter what happens to us as individuals.

Prison life is hard and stifling. All the while I am in jail, I cannot help thinking of my comrades who are being hounded and hunted as desperadoes—men of the finest mettle and devotion to the highest interests of the American people. The same Department of Justice that hounds them watches with silent acceptance while the big politicians raid the Treasury of the U.S, accept all matter of graft, head the biggest dope rackets, lynch Negroes and commit the most heinous crimes. Not only do these real criminals escape punishment, but often they are promoted to the highest office.

What was to be my attitude in jail—towards my fellow inmates and towards the prison officials? I had certain general ideas on the subject, but they were too sketchy to be useful. I had spoken to several of our comrades and other progressives who had "done time." But after a few weeks in Terre Haute, I discovered I had not talked enough. Our party people had always been too busy fighting for the other political prisoners—from Tom Mooney to the Scottsboro Boys—to give much consideration to how we ourselves would act as prisoners.

Towards the other inmates I felt that they, too, were victims of the prison system, as I was, and I expected them to look upon me in the same manner. On the whole, this is what happened—with some exceptions, of course. I soon learned that the primary thing on a prisoner's mind is the date of his release. And since this was my prime consideration, there was at least one preoccupation common to all of us.

Actually, most of my attitudes and views in prison had to be worked out as I went along. About many things I was inexcusably naïve. It worked both ways: I was surprised at some of the things one could do, and even more amazed at some of the things one couldn't. An example of the latter was that if one lived in a cell block, one had to get an officer's permit to take a shower. Most of these surprises, however, were about the little things. And all the while one thing remained clearly etched in my mind—my class was the working class and it was the ruling class that had put me in jail.

Marx had said that a Communist must be interested in all the phenomena of life. If this is true for things, it is a million times more true for people. And in prison there are many, many types of people—from thwarted geniuses to inflated halfwits. It was interesting to observe and study some of them—evidently not an unusual pastime among prisoners. I was once, for example, surprised to learn that I had been observed by one of the prisoners and that he had concluded that I was no Communist because I had a sense of humor. I replied, "your idea of communist comes from the papers and the radio. Communists love life and specialize in good humor."

I learned, too, from the prisoners—sometimes unwittingly. Two of three of us drifted into a discussion of war one day, and they wanted to know my attitude. For about ten of 15 minutes I patiently explained my views, going into some detail. When I finished, rather pleased with myself, one of them asked bluntly: "Well, are you for or against war?" For a moment I was stunned. But the truth was that I had used language, qualifications and the fine shadings that only one as accustomed as I was to political discussion could possibly have understood me. I thought I was making myself clear, but I suspected that maybe my virtues as a popular speakers were somewhat overrated.

One gets news of all kinds in jail. Some of it has the impact of a bombshell. The news of Mother Bloor's death stunned me, although I knew that the last few of her 88 years had been very trying of her. Nevertheless, no one who had worked with her and learned to love and appreciate her could possibly be prepared for her death. She was one of the most truly great women this country has produced. She possessed a stout heart, an unquenchable fighting spirit, and a total devotion to the American working class and the poor farmers. Her love for people and for our party was as big as the seven seas. The mother of several children, some of them distinguished men and women, she nevertheless considered all of us as her sons and daughters and treated us that way. What a personification of the eternal youth of a fighting Communist! Her personality was always refreshing, her wit ready, her tongue sharp against the enemies of our party and the working class. I saw and heard her speak about a year and a half before her death, and even then her mind was as clear as a bell—in much better condition that her ailing body. Mother Bloor and her leadership were a living inspiration to the millions of working Americans.

When I first became a member of the party, her words of encouragement had a great deal to do with my initiation into the spirit of brotherhood that prevails between Negro and white in the organization. Her sensitivity to the triple oppression of Negro women was boundless—I felt her loss as a deeply personal one.

When I had been in prison four months, my sister informed me of the death of my uncle, John Davis. I was saddened by this news, too, though I had not seen Uncle John in about 15 years and we had not been together very much since I was a boy in my early teens. But I remember him vividly. He had helped to rear my sister and me. He must have been in his late nineties at his death, and though wizened with age, he must have had a tough constitution— he never seemed to grow old. He was born in slavery, remembered his master, and used to relate the experiences of slavery and Reconstruction days to my sister and me. The other of my father's brothers, he was a carpenter and remained active at his trade until he was eighty. He wasn't particularly political-minded, but if he thought he had a point, he would stand his ground until the cows came home. One of the delights of my sister and me when we were kids was to see Uncle John and our father get into a heated argument. My father, who had a brilliant mind and a fierce, indomitable will, would shout every argument under the sun at his brother and should have won by all the laws of logic and debate. But Uncle John would stick to his guns—never raising his voice and refusing to be intimidated. Often father would quit in sheer exasperation but Uncle John never quit. We admired father's brilliance, but our sympathies were with Uncle John. . . .

In addition to other diversions, I sought relief in the performance of normal prison duties. For example, our cells were subject to frequent official inspections. At such times one was required to have his cell in perfect order and cleanliness. This meant cleaning beds, bowls, sweeping, scouring, dusting, and polishing everything within reach. Bon Ami and I struck up an acquaintance that was to find us inseparable throughout my term. I would apply myself with gusto to various tasks—anything to break the monotony.

But notwithstanding all the diversions and interests I could summon, nothing would relieve for long the natural oppressive atmosphere of prison, and the gnawing pain of being deprived of one's right to daily living and struggling. What I have written here with respect to my experiences in prison applies not only to Terre Haute but to the entire system, which I have evaluated; so far as I could, in the light on my Marxist outlook. I have given the reactions of a man unjustly in prison because of his political opinions. I agree with Mr. Justice Black and Mr. Justice Douglas that the imprisonment of me and my Communist colleagues under the Smith Act constitutes a monstrous violation of the Bill of Rights—particularly the First Amendment. In view of this, there is no jail that could be anything but hateful to me. I am not a criminal, not a menace to anyone. The real criminals, the real menace to the American people are the monopolies that are shoving our country down the road towards disaster, suffering, atomic war and fascism. As much as I value my freedom and resent being robbed of it, the crime against the peace and liberties of the American people is far more sinister.

Social revolutions are not made by Communists; they are made by capitalists who become so corrupt that they leave the people no basis for confidence in them, and the people have no recourse but to replace the system that breeds such suffering and privation. Communism is the science of replacing that system with a just and decent society.

Louise Thompson Patterson

Louise Alone Thompson Patterson (1901–1999), born on September 9, 1901, in Chicago, graduated in 1923 with honors from the University of California, Berkeley, with a degree in economics. That was no mean achievement for a woman of color in those days. Soon afterward, she taught at the Hampton Institute in Virginia but chafed under the domination of white paternalists; then she journeyed to New York, where she studied social work. She met a number of noted Harlem Renaissance writers and began a lifelong friendship with the poet Langston Hughes. She worked on several projects with Hughes and his artistic collaborator, Zora Neale Hurston. Louise's apartment in New York City was a well-known center of black cultural activity (salon) during the Harlem Renaissance. She became involved in several projects during this time, including the controversial and unrealized Soviet film project Black and White, *which looked at black life in the United States. During the 1930s, this young black radical also worked on behalf of the Scottsboro defendants in one of the most noted cause célèbre legal trials of racial injustice during the decade.*

By 1935, Patterson was working for the Communist-associated group known as the International Workers' Order (IWO). Organized into units based on ethnic identity and providing low-cost insurance and other benefits to its members, the IWO also fostered political awareness through its newspapers and social halls. In 1938, Patterson and Langston Hughes founded the Harlem Suitcase Theatre. The touring company, funded by the IWO to provide a forum for African American playwrights, presented Hughes's Don't You Want to Be Free? *as its debut performance.*

In 1940, Patterson married her longtime friend and comrade William L. Patterson, a black leader in the American Communist Party. In Chicago, the duo worked for the IWO on the city's black South Side. In 1947, when the U.S. attorney general ordered the IWO to disband, the radical couple threw themselves into the founding of the Civil Rights Congress (CRC). For about a decade, with the help of the Pattersons, the CRC expanded to some 10,000 members. It also lobbied for civil-rights legislation, publicized causes of racial injustice in the South, defended Communists prosecuted during the McCarthy era, and provided a training ground for many of the leaders of the civil-rights protests of the 1960s.

During the second half of the twentieth century, Louise Patterson kept busy with radical causes, including the defense of Angela Davis during the 1970s. She was widowed in 1980 and died in a New York nursing home on August 27, 1999.

■ ■ ■

The Soviet Film

The Crisis, February 1933

In the current issue of THE CRISIS I noticed a statement of your not having seen any satisfactory explanation of the postponement of the film "Black and White," for the making of which a group of twenty-two Negroes was invited to the Soviet Union last June [1932].

It is quite true that such statements have not been given such publicity in the white capitalist press of America as have the false allegations of complete abandonment of the picture for political reasons. The reason must be obvious to you, knowing as you do the attitude of this press to the Negro, as well as to the Soviet Union. Many statements have been issued collectively and individually by the majority of our group and have been steadily ignored by the representatives of the press through whom the adverse statements were released. Eugene Lyons, the United Press correspondent in Moscow, refused to send out the statement signed by fifteen members of our group repudiating the charges of four of our number which he had readily cabled over the wires of the United Press service.

I am sure you realize that the capitalist press is especially eager to discredit in the eyes of American Negroes the one country in the whole world which gives them complete equality—the only country that has successfully solved the national question. Pre-revolution Russia was called the "prison of nations" with over one hundred different minor nationalities held in oppression by the Great Russians who deliberately fostered national antagonisms to "divide and conquer." Today the Soviet government has proved in its untangling of these national snarls that its national policy—the right of self-determination for minor nationalities, the economic development of their backward regions, and the encouragement of national culture—is a correct one.

The matter of the postponement of a film is something which occurs daily in Hollywood or other film centers. Scenario and technical difficulties are not mysterious, political intrigues in any place but the Soviet Union. In the case of this film, the facts of its postponement are very simple to understand, once one divorces them from the entanglement of bourgeois propaganda against the Soviet Union.

The heart of the difficulty was in Meschrabpom-Film's sending for our group before the necessary preparations for the production of the picture had been completed in the Soviet Union. The scenario was neither complete nor approved, and the German director, Karl Junghaus, worked intensively on it, after our arrival in Moscow, to try to get it ready to begin work. Langston Hughes, a member of our group, was asked to help in this work of scenario revision, and he later participated in the conference where this revised scenario was presented for approval. The conference ended with no agreement being reached about the scenario. Meanwhile, the director Junghaus had declared that if work on the picture did not begin by August 15, it would have to be postponed until next year because of winter weather conditions. After that date there was nothing to do but to postpone work for this year.

"Black and White" is on the calendar of productions of Meschrabpom-Film for 1933, with work to begin between June and August. Those members of our group who returned to the United

States are invited to return to the Soviet Union to participate in the film, with the probable addition of others.

Another point which should be clarified is the matter of confusion of Meschrabpom-Film with the Soviet government. Meschrabpom-Film is not a Soviet but an international organization, the Workers' International Relief, with international headquarters in Berlin. There are American, German, French, British and other national divisions of this organization. We were invited to the Soviet Union by Meschrabpom-Film and all our subsequent relations were with this organization. Consequently, to confuse the actions of Meschrabpom-Film in postponing the picture with any action on the part of the Soviet government is to consciously distort the truth of the matter.

It is extremely ironical and unfortunate that four Negroes, who, for the first time in their lives enjoyed complete equality in Soviet Russian, should walk into the trap of becoming the weapon against the Soviet Union of those capitalist forces that oppress them in America.

Louise Thompson Patterson Papers, 1909–1999, Emory University Manuscript, Archives, and Rare Book Library, Atlanta, Georgia

Chapter 5: Return to America and Scottsboro

Unpublished Memoirs of Louise Thompson Patterson, Box 20, Folder No. 4, Memoirs. Series 4, Writings, 1930s–1990s.

I returned to the U.S. in November, 1932. Mother was very ill. I nursed her as best I could, demanding from her doctors some kind of medication that would relieve the tremendous pain that the cancer was causing her. She passed in February of the next year. It was a terrible thing, losing my mother. She had been a continuous, stable force throughout my life, and I knew that I would miss her terribly. But a part of me was relieved because there was no way out, and she had suffered so much. She died at seven o'clock in the morning. The drugs that they gave her had come to the point that they just crazed her, but did not ease her pain. So I was relieved for her sake. My reaction to losing her was to throw myself completely into my work.

I was still working for the Congregational Society. They had a great deal to do with financing my trip because my mother was ill; and in order for me to leave her with sufficient funds, I was away from June to November. The Department of Social Relations gave me several months' salary in advance. When I came back, my job was still open. I just didn't feel that I could go back to it because playing around with conferences, discussions which got nowhere, just seemed to me not to be the way to go. We would have seminars with largely white groups to raise their consciousness. I had organized a seminar through the South, which took the heads of various organizations—especially church organizations, like the head of the American Missionary Society which was in this group—and they were talking about the pioneers in developing black colleges in the South after slavery. Fred Brownley was a member of our seminar, as was Mrs. Bethune, perhaps the most distinguished member. We had discussions. We didn't touch the average white or black person.

I went back to the organization and had a talk with my director, and I told him that I just couldn't go back to that job because I felt I was not being sincere, that we had to take a much more fundamental approach. I had been asked by some of the leaders of the International Labor Defense (ILD) and a committee which had been set up to get people interested in the Scottsboro case to join forces with them. That is what I elected to do.

In 1931, America was in the very depths of the depression and there were hunger marches, marches of the unemployed, veterans were going to Washington, Hoovervilles all over the country, for it was the age of Herbert Hoover, until 1932, when Roosevelt took over. Wandering the countryside were groups of young people who were going from place to place, seeking work, and just going about. Many of them didn't have anything to do with the marches. At this particular instance, there was this train going through Alabama and a fight ensued between the blacks and whites on the train. This was probably provoked by the whites. They wired ahead about this trouble, and when they got to Scottsboro, the sheriffs were there and they found these black boys, nine black boys, in a boxcar and jailed them. Their ages were from 14 up to about 19. Roy Wright was the youngest boy, and he was either 13 or 14 years old.

They were railroaded through a trial and afterwards the officers found that there were two white girls, probably dressed in men's clothing, who were on the train in another car, and the story got around that they had been raped. The actual fact was, I think, that these were two prostitutes and they, in order to protect themselves, used a cry of rape. Of course, the boys were railroaded into the typical riot scene and mob scene, and they were all sentenced to die. They were arrested before any talk of rape.

There were organizers down in the South before the progressive organizations doing work, some of them working with sharecroppers and some of them working with other bodies, and they came to know about this trial and inform people in New York. At first, the boys were left defenseless. The NAACP had something to do with it, but I think they did not pick it up energetically. So the International Labor Defense did. The ILD was a left-wing group that had been active in cases like Sacco–Vanzetti but never before in anything that was of this nature, particularly with blacks, where the question of oppression of black people came into the picture. It so happens that the leader of this organization at that point was my husband to be some years later, William L. Patterson. He was a native Californian who was a lawyer who had come into the progressive movement.

The ILD began to take up the case and started getting other lawyers and demanding a new trial. They began to organize on an entirely new basis, not just as a courtroom trial, but in getting mass support by mobilizing people and by having meetings and rallies and so forth. As this happened, groups like the miners down in Kentucky, the textile workers in Jersey and New England, and the Sacco–Vanzetti case had brought a great many intellectuals into the field. A committee was then organized called "The National Committee for the Defense of Political Prisoners," which had Theodore Dreiser as its chairman. It was comprised of some of the leading intellectuals, probably more whites than blacks. That was the organization that I was invited to come into and be an Assistant Director. My activities were to be primarily those of mobilizing black people behind the defense. Our headquarters was downtown at 11th and Broadway, 799 Broadway. I opened the Harlem office which was located in a storefront on 135th St., near the YMCA. We had an all-black staff of about three of four people.

One of our first activities became that of mobilizing the people to march on Washington, D.C. Most of the established organizations like the NAACP or the Civil Liberties Committee never did that kind of thing. The only group that I know of who had that type of activity was the International Labor Defense. There could have been some others in the labor field, but I am not quite sure of that. In the Sacco–Vanzetti case there were many delegations that went to Boston around that case, but they did not get the man-on-the-street involved. We organized it so that we would try to get the people in Harlem involved in going to Washington en masse. We had to raise some money for the buses, and so my first job was something I had never done in my life, organize a mass protest march on Washington. I think we worked about two or three months to do this.

The morning of the day we were to take off, 135th St. was roped in between Lenox and Seventh. The buses were brought in, and the people came out and got on the buses. Every age group was represented, men and women. It was something. People came with children, cripples came, old people came, and we didn't have enough buses for all of them to fit in. We had to get some more buses, and instead of getting off on our journey in the morning, we didn't leave until 1 P.M. It was quite a thrill. We organized this by creating a committee, and we had meetings with churches, we put out leaflets, we had the office right on the street level. The committee was predominantly made up of black members, but I am sure there were also some whites. The object was to mobilize the people. My job was to arouse the people of Harlem to go to Washington.

The first night we got as far as Philadelphia, ninety miles. When we got to Philadelphia, we were put up in a church. The church prepared food for us. The next day we got as far as Baltimore, and we spent the night there. Then the next day we made it to Washington. I can remember, when we got to Washington, we had, I guess, the whole police squad and motorcycle squads out in force. They were along each side as we got off the buses and marched into the city. They had us enclosed on both sides with motor cops, who let their exhaust fumes out into the faces of the people. But we made it! I think that the most remarkable thing was that we had no accidents or incidents; nobody got sick. We got all of those people into Washington and home to New York without incident.

We had a big meeting in a park in Washington. I don't know which park. We picked up people along the way, in Baltimore, Philadelphia, and, of course Washingtonians came along too. In a way it was a mixed bag of emotions for me to be part of this. It was exciting.

ALTERNATIVE DESCRIPTION to March on Washington:

My assignment was to get the black people involved in the struggle for freedom of the Scottsboro Boys. Now, the committed itself was made up primarily of white intellectuals, and taking the office to Harlem was an effort to reach out and touch the common people, the working class people. Not that there was any ban on also getting intellectuals interested, but we wanted to get the masses of people involved. Perhaps it seems strange today when it is normal for the NAACP to call on people to mobilize and March in Washington. At that time these were considered communist methods. Taking the issue to the streets was not considered to be the way to carry on struggle. The Sixties, of course, changed all that. But in 1933, that was not the message that the NAACP and like organizations were putting down. It's true that all during the struggle for the Scottsboro Boys, especially many of the black churches and the ministers had been involved. There had been Father Bishop of St. Episcopal Church in Harlem on 133rd Street. Adam Clayton Powell had had mass meetings at Abyssinian. But still, taking it to the streets in organizing a march on Washington was unheard of.

The first thing I did was get an office up in Harlem. At that time 135th St., and not 125th St., was the center of black activity. There was a library on 135th Street; the YMCA was on 135th Street. St. Phillips Church had a housing development on 133rd St. Abyssinia Church was on 138th St. The YWCA was on 137th St. All of these community organizations were pretty much between Lenox Avenue and Seventh or Eighth Avenues. So we wanted to center our activities right in the center of life in Harlem. The next thing was to staff the office. We had about two to three young black women who worked with us in the office. And then, of course, we had to get a committee in Harlem to sponsor and to help mobilize the people. And that was my first activity. I had never been involved in organizing any mass movement. But there were many who helped me, and so that began the work. It was very interesting. We had a storefront, so people could come in and find out all the information. We also had to raise funds because the people we were mobilizing didn't have any money. We solicited contributions so that we could get charter buses for the march to Washington.

Of course, we had to be in touch with other cities, particularly Philadelphia and Baltimore and Washington, because our effort was to mobilize the Eastern Seaboard; it was not at that point a national effort. We did not try to organize the march only for left people. We were getting the masses of people and the churches. Remember that at the same time the Depression was in full effect, so there were the unemployment councils and other organizations of people who were struggling to better their conditions who joined in willingly.

When the day finally came, the block between Lenox and Seventh, which was the main thoroughfare, was blocked off. There was no traffic on that block. The buses came, and the people came. Where they came from, I don't even know, but the buses that had been ordered were so promptly filled up that we had to get many more buses. The streets, the whole block was just like a huge mass gathering itself. And people of every category were there: old people, young people, mothers with babies in their arms, children. It was something else. I think it actually frightened me when I saw what was happening. We started mobilizing early in the morning, maybe around 7:00 [A.M.] or so, and we weren't able to pull away, to start for Washington, until about 1:00 o'clock in the afternoon. I didn't ride in the bus because I wanted to be able to travel back and forth and see what was going on, so I traveled by car. I don't remember whether we picked up people en route between Harlem and Philadelphia or not. I think we left solidly packed from Harlem. But by the time we got to Philadelphia, and that's only 90 miles, it was already dark. I can't recall the names of the churches, but a large Baptist Church had prepared food, and people slept on the pews and on the benches in the church. There were not enough beds.

Then we had to get up the next morning and start out. And the second day we made Baltimore, which was probably 100 miles. And we stayed in Baltimore all night, under similar circumstances. And the third morning, we got up and made the 45 miles to

Washington, D.C. Just imagine, all these people, of all ages, all sizes, in various degrees of capacity to mobility.

We had huge meetings, and as Scottsboro caught on the people began to respond to our efforts. Then the politicians started trying to get a piece of the pie. And I can recall a tremendous meeting that was held in Brooklyn, in the Brooklyn Academy of Music, and all of the wards, all of the politicians, black and white, turned out for that meeting. William L. Patterson was on the platform. They had a white woman, political committee woman or something like that, the kind of people who would never have anything to do with Scottsboro, out there speaking. And I can remember that William Paterson was so mad, angry, [and] cried, because when the time came for him, the leader of the ILD, to speak, all of the people had left the hall—because it was after midnight. So the next mass big meeting was held in Abyssinia Baptist Church in Harlem, and the church was packed to the rafters. Well, that same woman, white woman politician, was there. Pat got up and wiped the floor with her. He was quite an orator, you know, and when he got the floor that night, and he got it early, he whipped it, talking about the Johnny-come-lately's and the people who were trying to do this to advance their own political careers. He had her in tears. The General Secretary of the International Labor Defense did a spectacular job—to the point that he lost his health and collapsed with Tuberculosis in 1934. He had to go to the Soviet Union for three years, to recuperate and regain his health.

The International Labor Defense began to work with the families and to get the families to directly participate in the struggle to free their children. The two mothers that I got to know quite well were Mrs. Ada Wright and Mrs. Patterson (I think her first name was Jennie). Mrs. Wright was a very alert person, and very determined to fight for the lives of her two boys, Roy, the youngest, and his brother.

When they first came to New York, I was living at 409 Edgecombe, and had enough room so that they stayed with me, and I got to know both of these women quite well. Mrs. Patterson used to sit very quietly for a long time, looking out the window. I don't know that I ever knew what she was thinking about. I remember she used to chew snuff. And she'd have a can, tin can, and she'd sit by the window for hours, spitting into that improvised spittoon and thinking. But when it came time to go to the meeting or whatever they had to do, they did it.

Two things I'd like to say about Mrs. Wright. When we think about slavery, we remember the role that Frederick Douglass played in going to England and France in gaining the support of the British working class people. I had occasion to see when I was there in 1972 or 1973, that they were monuments up in industrial towns of London of workers who had come out in defense of, in support of the Union during the Civil War and where Frederick Douglass spoke. I think of Mrs. Wright in that way. Here was this simple country woman who was taken to Europe and addressed masses of people in many different countries. The man who took her was Secretary at that time of the International Labor Defense, which was the organization that had been set up by the left-wing forces to fight for civil rights and for both black and white. They were very active in the fight to save Sacco and Vanzetti. And the Scottsboro case, I think, was the first major case the International Labor Defense took up to struggle against the oppression of black people.

At a later point in the defense of the civil rights, of the Scottsboro Boys, there came a cleavage between the forces that supported the NAACP, which originally had come in but had not done much about the defense of the boys, but later on as the struggle got broader, came back into the case, but yet did not support the policies that the International Labor Defense was taking, of making it as a mass struggle, of making demonstrations as we had in Washington of picketing. Their policy at that point was to leave it as a legal fight. So at one point there was the struggle to get the families and the victims in Scottsboro to end their participation with the International Labor Defense and come under the NAACP. So when the break took place, I happened to be in the South then. By that time, I had left the National Committee and was working for the International Workers Order (IWO).

In the midst of the split, carrying on the campaign and getting organizations, the funds grew low. Now we didn't get paid very much in the ILD in the National Committee. But that was the only income I had at that point. I think I was making $25 a week, which enabled me to pay my rent and buy my food. But there was a lull in the campaign, and the sources of contributions rather died out. And, of course, the expenses of caring on the campaign itself were great. So I found that there were no funds, and I had nobody to fall back on. For the first time in my life, I began to fall back in my rent payments and didn't have any money to live on. But I felt that I had to do something about the situation—not that my interest was dimmed in the Scottsboro [case], but at least I had to have some money to live on. So I inquired among friends of mine whom I had made on the left, and a suggestion was made that maybe I could go to work for the International Workers Order because it was a business, not a charitable organization. The International Workers Order was a fraternal insurance society made up of 16 different national groups, ethnic groups. The base of the organization was its insurance. Therefore, it did not depend upon voluntary contributions. They had a business to run. So you got paid.

So I went to work for them as a clerical worker, to begin with. But I didn't stay very long as a clerical worker because I was sitting there writing these policies, and seeing people paying and getting a policy for thousand dollars or two thousand dollars or three thousand dollars, and I began to think, well, this is something the black people should be interested in. Because black people, I got to know, as I was around working in the South on Scottsboro, even around in the black community, and down in Birmingham, could never afford adequate insurance. And what little they could manage was doled out in demeaning ways. I remember that in every black neighborhood, one day a week you would see these white insurance agencies weaving their way through the black community, coming to the door, never taking off their hats: "Is Maggie in?" Standing there in all of their arrogance and white supremacy and collecting the nickels, dimes, quarters or fifty cent pieces from black folk that netted them a policy anywhere from $100–$150. So they never had a kind of insurance that would be adequate even to bury them, to leave something for the families. It was a scandal. When I went to New York and saw that Metropolitan Life building down on 23rd and Madison, I thought, "This is the building that black workers built." The industrial policies were practically the only insurance that any of them ever had.

So I spoke to some of the leaders of the IWO. I was just there as a clerical worker at my $25 a week and paying my rent. At that time you could get a fairly decent apartment in Harlem for $50–$60 a month. So I began to look at these things, and I saw that there were certainly no blacks in there. I spoke to some of the organizers, the leaders of the organization. I said, "You know, I'd like to see black people get into this organization." I didn't sit at a desk and write policies very long before I was made an organizer, and my first track was down South.

Now, Samuel Leibowitz had been brought into the case before the new trial, by William Patterson. Pat felt that Leibowitz was the best man for the case because he was one of the best trial lawyers in the country. And he knew that when the new trial took place, down in the South, they would have to have a strong lawyer who, first of all, would dare to go down there and secondly, would dare to make a fight in the classroom. This move on the part of the ILD and William Patterson split the National Committee for the Defense of Political Prisoners, with which I was identified. I was the assistant director. But the director and many friends, including people like Lionel and Diana Trilling, who were among the very bitter anti-Communist and anti-Soviet forces in the intellectual world at that time, withdrew from the National Committee with the defense of political prisoners because they felt it was wrong to take a lawyer who had been the foremost gangster's lawyer, known as such, and bring him into the fight. Pat's answer was, . . . "I don't give a heck what his background is, if he can win in the court room in Decatur, Alabama."

Leibowitz, after all, was an opportunist. He was trying to make his name, and I think what he felt here was legitimate, accepted, respected in the NAACP, and maybe I'll have better luck than I did with the ILD. So he jumped ship to go with the NAACP. My job was to counter his influence.

So I jumped in my car, and it was a young black man, I don't even remember his name at this point, a hitchhiker, whom I picked up along the way and helped me with my driving. We left one night and went from Atlanta to Memphis. I remember that drive, because we had to go through a lot of valleys, and fog. He was driving almost blind. We drove all night to get to Memphis. Well, the first home I went to was the home of Ada Wright, the next day. I guess I went to their house and stayed with them. And I went out to where Ada was working to fetch her after her work day was over. Ada was working there for $5 a week. Cooking, cleaning that big house, taking care of the children, doing the washing and ironing, $5 a week. And I don't think they paid her car fare. So you can see the conditions under which people were living there. She was working in the white neighborhood. It was a huge house. I can remember it was a big old white house in the white neighborhood. I guess I went to the front door. I'm sure I didn't go round to the kitchen as most had to do. And Ada came out, and her boss came out. He was going somewhere, and I asked him would he want a ride. So Ada got in the car, and he got in the car, and we started back to go to the black community to her house. And he started talking to me. He said, "You know, I don't mind if Ada teams up with you, you folks, I've no objection about it." "But," he said, "the thing is you gotta tell her not to be sassy." He said "not to talk back" and to "stay in her place." He said, "If she does that, I don't have no objection at all what you are all doing because those boys should be free." Now, that was a liberal!

I went back to her house, and I spent the night. I went to bed, and suddenly I woke up. I didn't know what was happening. I was sleeping in the living room with one of the children. I looked up, and turned on the light to see what was happening, and the bed bugs were walking up and down the walls like an army. I get out of that bed and sat up for the rest of the night, and the child I was sleeping with never woke up. You know, I had been poor all my life, but I was seeing conditions that I had never, never, never seen in my life.

Well, I had no trouble with Ada. I arrived in time. Terry was there. And I went over to the Pattersons. There were two families, the Pattersons and the Wrights. And I saw Mrs. Patterson. Well, she said, "I can't go cuz [sic] I got to stay here to take care of my granddaughter, Louise," her name was. (They said "Lou-ise.") I begged her, got down on my knees to beg her to go. She wouldn't go. Terry had gotten the father, the Patterson father, to agree to go with him. And they were at the train. I jumped in the car and went down to the station, and there was Terry with Mr. Patterson, and the train was just about to pull out. As it tried to pull out, I tried to pull that man off the train. Oh, I was just heartbroken. The train went on out, and the only one Terry had was Mr. Patterson. Well, I think I went back and worked on Mrs. Patterson. I got on my knees, and I cried, and begged her to go with me, told her what it means. So finally I got her and Ada Wright to come to demonstrate, and we left out that night, to go down to Montgomery, where the boys were in Kilby prison.

Now, Terry had to go by train to Birmingham, and then change trains to go down to Montgomery. So me and my little company got in the car about midnight and drove all night long, racing against the train time, through all that fog and mist, and got to Montgomery the next morning, about 8:00 o'clock. We beat Terry there because he had to wait for the train. Ben Davis had been sent down by the ILD to counsel with the boys, and I took my party over to Ben Davis and turned them over to him, so that when Terry got there with Mr. Patterson, Ben Davis was there with the Scottsboro mothers.

I was no stranger to these women, because I wasn't just someone coming from the North. They had slept in my house, eaten my food, and I had traveled with them around to meetings. So I think they had confidence in me. And, of course, I knew them much better than the father, and it was the women who played the major role in the defense of their sons. And so it was. Terry was real surprised to see us there because the last thing he had seen of me was my trying to pull Mr. Patterson off the train.

While I was in the South, I found that this struggle became the symbol for any fighting for civil rights. The people down South kept saying "Yes, I'm a member of the ILD." And ILD became symbolic of the struggle.

What did this case symbolize? One thing I think was very important was the role of Ruby Bates, one of the so-called victims of the Scottsboro boys. We had always been taught, I mean black people, that the enemy was poor whites, and that they were poor white trash, and that the boss was the good white man. Ruby Bates and Victoria Price were known as prostitutes. This case, in a sense, exploded that myth about rape and exposed some of the forces that were behind it—that poor whites could be used as the agent to do the lynching, but behind it stood the state, its courts, its police, the whole government, in terms of oppression of the black people. Now I'm not saying that this came clearly out in every instance. But when Ruby Bates made that trip from the South and spoke at that first meeting of the 66th Street hall in New York City, the air was so electric that night, if you had scratched the match, I think it would have exploded to see this young white girl march up there and say that these black boys didn't do it. That was the first time that we know of in history. Some whites got to her to convince her to tell the truth. And there was enough decency in her heart that she had to be honest. She hadn't been completely corrupted. Victoria Price, the other woman, on the other hand, was a hussie, and she never repudiated her first testimony. Ruby, however, had stayed with me at times. I got to know her well. And she was a decent person who wasn't ready to kill nine black boys who didn't rape her. She finally left New York after the case was over and all; she had to stay out of the South, of course. The last I heard of her she was in Minnesota. She married someone. She had a lot of guts. And certainly Pat was right in saying that Leibowitz was good, because he had guts. I don't know that he had scruples, but he had guts. Finally, at the end, there was some kind of compromise made, the NAACP eventually came back into the case.

Amazingly, about a year later, in 1934, I found myself in the same jail with three of the Scottsboro Boys. And one of the girls in my cell block claimed to be the sweetheart of one of the Wright boys. She used to get notes from them. In those days, organizing in the South, amongst the rest of the activists, you would get involved at any facet of the struggle that happened to be current at the moment. It so happened at that point, when I was in Birmingham, the uppermost struggle at that point was a strike in the mines. Now Birmingham (and I've been in many Southern cities) was the meanest town I've ever seen in in my life. Both the class and caste struggle were sharper there. I was there during May Day, and the tradition was, from a labor point of view, to have a rally of workers. I went down to the May Day rally to help hand out leaflets. Do you know, when you got downtown they didn't let two Negroes assemble together?! If blacks were on the street, they had to move. They did not permit anybody to stop. Do you know in the office buildings they had machine guns pointed down from the windows to where the rally was supposed to be held? Now, the main union there was the miners' union, and, contrary to all the other unions that I know and to the credit of John L. Lewis, blacks and whites were organized in the same locals. It's the only union like that that I knew in the South, and they were out and steadfast in terms of the strike. The papers were full of the news of the strike. But of course, as with anything else, any kind of people's struggle, the newspapers claimed it was the Reds that were doing it and not the grievances of the miners. Well my work for the IWO was akin to the labor movement; we were interested in working with workers and giving them the benefits of our program. So I became interested in the strike. I had to. I went to strike meetings. And one night I went out, Endsley or some place, the Red Mountain, they used to call it, and attended one of these meetings, and there were important elements in the strike, some important knowledge that I wanted to get to some of my progressive friends. It had nothing to do with IWO, but it had to do with the workers, and their program and their struggle.

So the next day I tried to reach these friends, who were communists, and I couldn't find anybody. So I knew of a woman who was editing and publishing the *Southern Worker,* who was white, and I knew where she was, and I thought, "If I get hold of Elizabeth, she'll know where people are." She had done a great deal of writing about the South, and she wrote quite a bit. She was well acquainted and versed in Negro history. So I decided I'd go visit her, and see, and try to get the message across, and what I knew about where the strike was and some people I knew. Well, I was living with a middle class black family whose relatives I knew in Harlem. They used to worry about me. They'd say, "We don't like you going out by yourself." They'd never seen a young black woman doing this kind of activity. And they said, "We have a friend who has a lot of time, and he'd be glad to take you around, because we just don't like you going around like this. It's dangerous." I said, "All right," so that afternoon George came by, and I asked him would he drive me out to the white community, where this woman lived. He said, "Sure." Well, what I did was leave him, fortunately, several blocks away, and told him to wait for me. And I got out and walked, and I walked into this middle class neighborhood to an apartment building, and knocked on the door. It was opened by a policeman. There was a raid going on! Elizabeth, the woman I was trying to contact, quickly said, "We don't have any sewing for you today." The policeman said, "That don't hold." He said, "We know you you're one of them Goddamn Yankee bitches from New York. Come on in here." So I walked into a raid. And when they came to take us away, they took all the whites and they put them in a paddy wagon, and they put me in a car. When this old white policeman took me out to the car, he said, "Daughter, what are you doing getting mixed up in a mess like this?" He said, "You know, [the] only thing wrong with these communists is they just like niggers too well. You shouldn't be involved in it." He just couldn't imagine a young black woman walking into a raid. So that's how I got jailed, and that's all it needed.

I WAS DETERMINED that I was not going to expose the people I lived with to anything, because, as I told them later, I said, "You have to live here." One was in the Post Office, one was a school teacher, one was a social worker—it was that kind of family. So I was determined that, no matter what it took, I would never let them know. I gave a false name, a false address, and I guess the word got spread around on the grapevine that I was in jail. It was even in the newspaper. There were about 50 of us black women in this very primitive wooden county jail the first night. Cots on each side. I had never seen a jail.

The next night they put me in this modern prison downtown, with the electric locked doors and the clicking of the steel as the door shut on your cell block. You had a cell block with about six individual cells were you slept. In the daytime you could come out to the general room, and that's where you ate, and socialized. They brought people up there to look at me like I was an animal on display. The white jailers did everything they could to insult me. They pretended they didn't know what I was saying when I spoke, and they couldn't understand my language. They had one of the Negro flunkies: when I turned around and stooped over for something, he hit me on my behind so they could laugh and sneer. When they were taking me to do the ID, I found myself in the elevator with the Sheriff, Bull Connor, who would become infamous in the 1960s. He pointed to me and said, "That's one of them goddamn Reds. They oughta do her like Mussolini does—take her out and shoot her against the wall."

I remember one of the girls in the first jail. She was a pickpocket. That night I spent my time finding out what crimes they were in for. All were black because, of course, it was a segregated jail. One was a pickpocket, one was a prostitute, one girl said she killed a man. I said, "What did you do? Shoot him?" She said, "No, Honey. I just put a knife right through his heart." The next morning when they came to get me to take me downtown to ID, Pinky, this big fat pickpocket, said to me, "Honey Jean" (I had given my name as "Jean"), "when you go down there, don't you be no goddamn fool. When that white man asks you a question, you say, 'yes sir; no, sir.' . . . That won't cost you nothin', Honey, but it'll save you plenty of hard knocks." Well, I got down there, and that white man started asking me questions, and I got so mad, I forgot all about Pinky. And when he stopped at one point and put his finger in my face and said, "Look here, gal, you're in the South now, and when I talk to you, you say, 'Yes sir, no sir.'" I was ready to die before "Sir" would cross my lips. I could not say "yes sir, no sir." The next question he asked me, I looked at him and I said, "No!" Now, I think the only thing that saved me those hard knocks was, first of all, these prison employees had probably never encountered a black woman like me. Secondly, between Scottsboro and the strike, Birmingham had so much on its hands, it didn't want to have any more cases to fight or defend themselves. And I think that's the only thing that saved me. Because at that point nobody, nobody in the wide world, knew where I was.

Birmingham was the most segregated place I was ever in. The streetcars, the whole atmosphere, was like nothing I had ever known. New Orleans wasn't like that. And Atlanta was not like that. In many of the Southern cities, they'd have a little sign that you could take off and move, depending on the number of blacks and whites in the streetcar at any given moment. But in Birmingham you had permanent boards that went from ceiling to floor that separated the sections. On some of the streetcars you had to get on the front, and pay your fare, then get off and walk to the back and get to your seat. You could not even walk through. They had three kinds of streetcars. One blacks had to get on in the back, one they had to get on in the middle, and one they had to get on in the front to pay their fare. So one day I used to be so mad when they'd be standing there waiting to get on that I'd say, "At least I'm going to be the first person on that streetcar; I don't care what happens." And I'd get up and get on first. So I didn't always know which kind of a streetcar I was on. So one day I got on, went to pay my fare, and I looked up, and this old, white conductor was sweating. And he looked at me and he said, "Please, ma'am, would you please tell me if you're colored or are you white?" I said, "I'm an American Negro." He said, "Well, will you please get off and go up to the front?" Tough days.

One night I was going to a left meeting. When you were down there, you knew everybody that's progressive; whether you're in the Communist Party or your ILD or you're in a labor organization or whatnot, you know people who are trying to bring about change in that area. So I was going to some meeting out in the industries on the outskirts of town. The guide who was supposed to tell me where to go was white. So we agreed that we'd go to this corner. I'd stand where I got on the streetcar, and he'd get on his where he was supposed to get off, and then we got to where we were going, he would get off one block, and I would get off the next. We stood on that street corner for almost an hour waiting for the streetcar, and he never looked at me and I never looked at him. When we got on the streetcar, I sat in my section and he sat in his, and then we got off. We did it the same way coming back. One got on and at one corner, one at the next corner. Unfortunately, we had the same conductor. He looked at me as if he were saying, "This is no accident." That's the kind of attention that you got. You could never relax, you were conscious every moment. I was scared because he really looked at me. Birmingham was the meanest town.

Nobody was convicted in the Scottsboro appeal trial. The Supreme Court ordered a new trial based on the conclusion that the defendants had not had adequate counsel in the first trial. The boys were sentenced to 99 years in prison in the new trial, but, by 1950, the last of them had been released. Most of them were never the same. I believe only one was able to lead the semblance of a normal life.

William L. Patterson

Born in San Francisco on August 27, 1891, William L. Patterson was a
Marxist attorney, writer, and civil-rights advocate. On his mother's side
of the family, he descended from Virginia slaves. Prior to the eruption of
the American Civil War, Patterson's mother was liberated and sent west
to California, where she met William's father. Rising from a poverty-
stricken background, young William graduated from high school in 1911
and attended the University of California for a time without graduating.

In 1915, Patterson enrolled at the Hastings College of Law (University of California, San Francisco). While attending law school, he began
to read The Crisis, the organ of the NAACP. Subsequently, he culti-
vated an interest in several Marxist and leftist publications, such as The
Masses and The Messenger. After earning a law degree in 1919, Patterson joined the NAACP.

Patterson also traveled to London after he graduated from law school
and briefly collaborated with Robert Lansbury of the London Daily
Times (British Labor Party). Inspired by an internationalist perspective
on race and class, Patterson returned to the United States, moved to New
York City, and threw himself into the fight for racial justice and equal
rights. As a crusading attorney for working-class African Americans and
immigrants, he worked on behalf of Nicola Sacco and Bartolomeo Vanzetti and the Scottsboro defendants.

Soon after World War II and the Holocaust, during the depths of the Cold War, Patterson stepped onto the international stage with his landmark study "We Charge Genocide," which he presented to the United Nations General Assembly in 1951. In the study, a remarkable historical document, the young black communist charged the U.S. government with the genocide of the African American people. His detailed analysis listed hundreds of instances of lynching, killing, bombing, and torture of African Americans in the nineteenth and twentieth centuries. It also offered countless, mind-numbing details of white racial crimes against blacks in all regions of the United States.

Patterson published other noteworthy works, including Ben Davis: Crusader for Negro Freedom and Socialism *and* The Man Who Cried Genocide. *During the 1960s, he defended Angela Davis and leaders of the Black Panther Party who were subjected to arrest. Patterson also served as executive secretary of the International Labor Defense and as a leader of the Civil Rights Congress, organizations that fought for African American rights. He died in New York City in 1980.*

▨ ▨ ▨

Tamiment Library and Robert F. Wagner Labor Archives,
New York University

We Charge Genocide

Excerpt from William L. Patterson, Civil Rights Congress (U.S.). *We Charge Genocide; The Historic Petition to the United Nations for Relief from a Crime of the United States Government against the Negro People* (New York: International Publishers, 1951; reprint 1970).

Introduction

Out of the inhuman black ghettos of American cities, out of the cotton plantations of the South, comes this record of mass slayings on the basis of race, of lives deliberately warped and distorted by the willful creation of conditions making for premature death, poverty and disease. It is a record that calls aloud for condemnation. For an end to these terrible injustices that constitute a daily and ever-increasing violation of the United Nations Convention on the Prevention and Punishment of the Crime of Genocide.

It is sometimes incorrectly thought that genocide means the complete and definitive destruction of a race or people. The Genocide Convention, however, adopted by the General Assembly of the United Nations on December 9, 1948, defines genocide as any killings on the basis of race, or, in its specific words, as "killing members of the group." Any intent to destroy, *in whole or in part*, a national, racial, ethnic or religious group is genocide, according to the Convention. Thus, the Convention states, "causing serious bodily or mental harm to members of the group" is genocide as well as "killing members of the group."

We maintain, therefore, that the oppressed Negro citizens of the United States, segregated, discriminated against and long the target of violence, suffer from genocide as the result of the consistent, conscious, unified policies of every branch of government.

The Civil Rights Congress has prepared and submits this petition to the General Assembly of the United Nations on behalf of the Negro people in the interest of peace and democracy, charging the Government of the United States of America with violation of the Charter of the United Nations and the Convention on the Prevention and Punishment of the Crime of Genocide.

We believe that in issuing this document we are discharging an historic responsibility to the American people, as well as rendering a service of inestimable value to progressive mankind. We speak of the American people because millions of white Americans in the ranks of labor and the middle class, and particularly those who live in the Southern states and are often contemptuously called poor whites, are themselves suffering to an ever-greater degree from the consequences of the Jim Crow segregation policy of the government in its relations with Negro citizens. We speak of progressive mankind because a policy of discrimination at home must inevitably create racist commodities for export abroad—must inevitably tend toward war.

We have not dealt here with the cruel and inhuman policy of this government toward the people of Puerto Rico. Impoverished and reduced to a semi-literate state through the wanton exploitation and oppression by gigantic American concerns, through the merciless frame-up and imprisonment of hundreds of its sons and daughter, this colony of the rulers of the United States reveals in all its stark nakedness the moral bankruptcy of this government and those who control its home and foreign policies.

History has shown that the racist theory of government of the U.S.A. is not the private affair of Americans, but the concern of mankind everywhere.

It is our hope, and we fervently believe that it was the hope and aspiration of every black American whose voice was silenced forever through premature death at the hands of racist-minded hooligans or Klan terrorists, that the truth recorded here will be made known to the world; that it will speak with a tongue of fire loosing an unquenchable moral crusade, the universal response to which will sound the death knell of all racist theories.

We have scrupulously kept within the purview of the Convention on the Prevention and Punishment of the Crime of Genocide which is held to embrace those "acts committed with intent to destroy in whole or in part a national, ethnical, racial or religious group as such."

We particularly pray for the most careful reading of this material by those who have always regarded genocide as a term to be used only where the acts of terror evinced an intent to destroy a whole nation. We further submit that this Convention on Genocide is, by virtue of our avowed acceptance of the Covenant of the United Nations, an inseparable part of the law of the United States of America.

According to international law, and according to our own law, the Genocide Convention, as well as the provisions of the United Nations Charter, supersedes, negates and displaces all discriminatory racist law on the books of the United States and the several States.

The Hitler crimes, of awful magnitude, beginning as they did against the heroic Jewish people, finally drenched the world in blood, and left a record of maimed and tortured bodies and devastated areas such as mankind had never seen before. Justice Robert H. Jackson, who now sits upon the United States Supreme Court bench, described this holocaust to the world in the powerful language with which he opened the Nuremberg trials of the Nazi leaders. Every word he voiced against the monstrous Nazi beast applies with equal weight, we believe, to those who are guilty of the crimes herein set forth.

Here we present the documented crimes of federal, state, and municipal governments in the United States of America, the dominant nation in the United Nations, against 15,000,000 of its own nationals—the Negro people of the United States. These crimes are of the gravest concern to mankind. The General Assembly of the United Nations, by reason of the United Nations Charter and the Genocide Convention, itself is invested with power to receive this indictment and act on it.

The proof of this fact is its action upon the similar complaint of the government of India against South Africa.

We call upon the United Nations to act and to call the Government of the United States to account.

We believe that the test of the basic goals of a foreign policy is inherent in the manner in which a government treats its own nationals and is not to be found in the lofty platitudes that pervade so many treaties or constitutions. The essence lies not in the form, but rather, in the substance.

The Civil Rights Congress is a defender of constitutional liberties, human rights, and of peace. It is the implacable enemy of every creed, philosophy, social system or way of life that denies democratic rights or one iota of human dignity to any human being because of color, creed, nationality or political belief.

We ask all men and women of good will to unite to realize the objectives set forth in the summary and prayer concluding this petition. We believe that this program can go far toward ending the threat of a third world war. We believe it can contribute to the establishment of a people's democracy on a universal scale.

But may we add as a final note that the Negro people desire equality of opportunity in this land where their contributions to the economic, political and social developments have been of splendid proportions and in quality second to none. They will accept nothing less, and continued efforts to force them into the category of second-class citizens through force and violence, through segregation, racist law and institutionalized oppression, can only end in disaster for those responsible.

Respectfully submitted by the Civil Rights Congress as a service to the peoples of the world, and particularly to the lovers of peace and democracy in the United States of America.

The Opening Statement

A review of the case and the Offer of Proof, giving something of the scope and historical background of the genocide being committed against the Negro people of the United States.

To the General Assembly of the United Nations

The responsibility of being the first in history to charge the government of the United States of America with the crime of genocide is not one your petitioners take lightly. The responsibility is particularly grave when citizens must charge their own government with mass murder of its own nationals, with institutionalized oppression and persistent slaughter of the Negro people in the United States on a basis of "race," a crime abhorred by mankind and prohibited by the conscience of the world as expressed in the Convention on the Prevention and Punishment of the Crime of Genocide adopted by the General Assembly of the United Nations on December 9, 1948.

Genocide Leads to Fascism and to War

If our duty is unpleasant it is historically necessary both for the welfare of the American people and for the peace of the world. We petition as American patriots, sufficiently anxious to save our countrymen and all mankind from the horrors of war to shoulder a task as painful as it is important. We cannot forget Hitler's demonstration that genocide at home can become wider massacre abroad, that domestic genocide develops into the larger genocide that is predatory war. The wrongs of which we complain are so much the expression of predatory American reaction and its government that civilization cannot ignore them nor risk their continuance without courting its own destruction. We agree with those members of the General Assembly who declared that genocide is a matter of world concern because its practice imperils world safety.

But if the responsibility of your petitioners is great, it is dwarfed by the responsibility of those guilty of the crime we charge. Seldom in human annals has so iniquitous a conspiracy been so gilded with the trappings of respectability. Seldom has mass murder on the score of "race" been so sanctified by law, so justified by those who demand free elections abroad, even as they kill their fellow citizens who demand free elections at home. Never have so many individuals been so ruthlessly destroyed amid so many tributes to the sacredness of the individual. The distinctive trait of this genocide is a cant that mouths aphorisms of Anglo-Saxon jurisprudence even as it kills.

The genocide of which we complain is as much a fact as gravity. The whole world knows of it. The proof is in every day's newspapers, in every one's sight and hearing in these United States. In one form or another it has been practiced for more than three hundred years although never with such sinister implications for the welfare and peace of the world as at present. Its very familiarity disguises its horror. It is a crime so embedded in law, so explained away by specious rationale, so hidden by talk of liberty, that even the conscience of mankind cannot by beguiled from its duty by the pious phrases and the deadly legal euphemisms with which its perpetrators seek to transform their guilt into high moral purpose.

Killing Members of the Group

Your petitioners will prove that the crime of which we complain is in fact genocide within the terms and meaning of the United Nations Convention providing for the prevention and punishment of this crime. We shall submit evidence, tragically voluminous, of "acts committed with intent to destroy, in whole or in part, a national, ethical, racial or religious group as such,"—in this case the 15,000,000 Negro people of the United States.

We shall submit evidence proving "killing members of the group," in violation of Article II of the Convention. We cite killings by police, killings by incited gangs, killings at night by masked men, killings always on the basis of "race," killings by the Ku Klux Klan, that organization which is chartered by the several states as a semi-official arm of government and even granted the tax exemptions of a benevolent society.

Our evidence concerns the thousands of Negroes who over the years have been beaten to death on chain gangs and in the back rooms of sheriff's offices, in the cells of country jails, in precinct police stations and on city streets, who have been framed and murdered by sham legal forms and by a legal bureaucracy. It concerns those Negroes who have been killed, allegedly for failure to say "sir" or tip their hats or move aside quickly enough, or, more often, on trumped up charges of "rape," but in reality for trying to vote or otherwise demanding the legal and inalienable rights and privileges of United States citizenship formally guaranteed them by the Constitution of the United States, rights denied them on the basis of "race," in violation of the Constitution of the United States, the United Nations Charter and the Genocide Convention.

Economic Genocide

We shall offer proof of economic genocide, or in the words of the Convention, proof of "deliberately inflicting on the group conditions of life calculated to bring about its destruction in whole or in part." We shall prove that such conditions so swell the infant and maternal death rate and the death rate from disease, that the American Negro is deprived, when compared with the remainder of the population of the United States, of eight years of life on the average.

Further we shall show a deliberate national oppression of these 15,000,000 Negro Americans on the basis of "race" to perpetuate these "conditions of life." Negroes are the last hired and the first fired. They are forced into city ghettos or their rural equivalents. They are segregated legally or through sanctioned violence into filthy, disease-bearing housing, and deprived by law of adequate medical care and education. From birth to death, Negro Americans are humiliated and persecuted, in violation of the Charter and the Convention. They are forced by threat of violence and imprisonment into inferior, segregated accommodations, into Jim Crow busses, Jim Crow trains, Jim Crow hospitals, Jim Crow schools, Jim Crow theaters, Jim Crow restaurants, Jim Crow housing, and finally into Jim Crow cemeteries.

We shall prove that the object of this genocide, as of all genocide, is the perpetuation of economic and political power by the few through the destruction of political protest by the many. Its method is to demoralize and divide an entire nation; its end is to increase the profits and unchallenged control by a reactionary clique. We shall show that those responsible for this crime are not the humble but the so-called great, not the American people but their misleaders, not the convict but the robed judge, not the criminal but the police, not the spontaneous mob but organized terrorists licensed and approved by the state to incite to a Roman holiday.

We shall offer evidence that his genocide is not plotted in the dark but incited over the radio into the ears of millions, urged in the glare of public forums by Senators and Governors. It is offered as an article of faith by powerful political organizations, such as the Dixiecrats, and defended by influential newspapers, all in violation of the United Nations charter and the Convention forbidding genocide.

This proof does not come from the enemies of the white supremacists but from their own mouths, their own writings, their political resolutions, their racists laws, and from photographs of their handiwork. Neither Hitler nor Goebbels wrote obscurantist racial incitements more voluminously or viciously than do their American counterparts, nor did such incitements circulate in Nazi mails any more freely than they do in the mails of the United States.

Conspiracy to Genocide

Through this and other evidence we shall prove this crime of genocide is the result of a massive conspiracy, more deadly in that it is sometimes "understood" rather than expressed, a part of the mores of the ruling class often concealed by euphemisms, but always directed to oppressing the Negro people. Its members are so well-drilled, so rehearsed over the generations, that they can carry out their parts automatically and with a minimum of spoken direction. They have inherited their plot and their business is but to implement it daily so that it works daily. This implementation is sufficiently expressed in decision and statute, in depressed wages, in robbing millions of the vote and millions more of the land, and in countless other political and economic facts, as to reveal definitively the existence of a conspiracy backed by reactionary interest in which are meshed all the organs of the Executive, Legislative and Judicial branches of government. It is manifest that a people cannot be consistently killed over the years on the basis of "race"—and more than 10,000 Negroes have suffered death—cannot be uniformly segregated, despoiled, impoverished and denied equal protection before the law, unless it is the result of the deliberate, all-pervasive policy of government and those who control it.

Emasculation of Democracy

We shall show, more particularly, how terror, how "killing members of the group," in violation of Article II of the Genocide Convention, has been used to prevent the Negro people from voting in huge and decisive areas of the United States in which they are the preponderant population, thus dividing the whole American people, emasculating mass movements for democracy and securing the grip of predatory reaction on the federal, state, county, and city governments. We shall prove that the crimes of genocide offered for your action and the world's attention have in fact been incited, a punishable crime under Article III of the Convention, often by such officials as Governors, Senators, Judges and peace officers whose phrases about white supremacy and the necessity of maintaining inviolate a white resulted in bloodshed as surely as more direct incitement.

We shall submit evidence showing the existence of a mass of American law, written as was Hitler's law solely on the basis of "race," providing for segregation and otherwise penalizing the Negro people, in violation not only of Articles II and III of the Convention but also in violation of the Charter of the United Nations. Finally we shall offer proof that a conspiracy exists in which the Government of the United States, its Supreme Court, its Congress, its Executive branch, as well as the various state, county and municipal governments, consciously effectuate policies which result in the crime of genocide being consistently and constantly practiced against the Negro people of the United States.

The Negro Petitioners

Many of your petitioners are Negro citizens to whom the charges herein described are not mere words. They are facts felt on our bodies, crimes inflicted on our dignity. We struggle for deliverance, not without pride in our valor, but we warn mankind that our fate is theirs. We solemnly declare that continuance of this American crime against the Negro people of the United States will strengthen those reactionary American forces driving towards World War III as certainly as the unrebuked Nazi genocide against the Jewish people strengthened Hitler in his successful drive to World War II.

We, Negro petitioners whose communities have been laid waste, whose homes have been burned and looted, whose children have been killed, whose women have been raped, have noted with peculiar horror that the genocidal doctrines and actions of the American white supremacists have already been exported to the colored peoples of Asia. We solemnly warn that a nation which practices genocide against its own nationals may not be long deterred, if it has the power, from genocide elsewhere. White supremacy at home makes for colored massacres abroad. Both reveal contempt for human life in a colored skin. Jellied gasoline in Korea and the lynchers' faggot at home are connected in more ways than that both result in death by fire. The lyncher and the atom bomber are related. The first cannot murder unpunished and unrebuked without so encouraging the latter that the peace of the world and the lives of millions are endangered. Nor is this metaphysics. The tie binding both is economic profit and political control. It was not without significance that it was President Truman who spoke of the possibility of using the atom bomb on the colored people of Asia, that it is American statesmen who prate constantly of "Asiatic hordes."

"Our Humanity Denied and Mocked"

We protest this genocide as Negroes and we protest it as Americans, as patriots. We know that no American can be truly free while 15,000,000 other Americans are persecuted on the grounds of "race," that few American can be prosperous while 15,000,000 are deliberately pauperized. Our country can never know true democracy while millions of its citizens are denied the vote on the basis of their color.

But above all we protest this genocide as human beings whose very humanity is denied and mocked. We cannot forget that after Congressman Henderson Lovelace Lanham, of Rome, Georgia, speaking in the halls of Congress, called William L. Patterson, one of the leaders of the Negro people, "a God-damned black son-of-bitch," he added, "We gotta keep the black apes down." We cannot forget it because this is the animating sentiment of the white supremacists, of a powerful segment of American life. We cannot forget that in many American states it is a crime for a white person to marry a Negro on the racist theory that Negroes are "inherently inferior as an immutable fact of Nature." The whole institution of segregation, which is training for killing, education for genocide, is based on Hitler-like theory of the "inherent inferiority of the Negro." The tragic fact of segregation is the basis for the statement, too often heard after murder, particularly in the South, "Why I think no more of killing a n—r, than of killing a dog."

We petition in the first instance because we are compelled to speak by the unending slaughter of Negroes. The fact of our ethnic origin, of which we are proud—our ancestors were building the world's first civilizations 3,000 years before our oppressors emerged from barbarism in the forests of western Europe—is daily made the signal for segregation and murder. There is infinite variety in the cruelty we will catalogue, but each case has the common denominator of racism. This opening statement is not the place to present our evidence in detail. Still, in this summary of what is to be proved, we believe it necessary to show something of the crux of our case, something of the pattern of genocidal murder, the technique of incitement to genocide, and the methods of mass terror.

Our evidence begins with 1945 and continues to the present. It gains in deadliness and in number of cases almost in direct ratio to the surge towards war. We are compelled to hold to this six years span if this document is to be brought into manageable proportions.

The Evidence

There was a time when racist violence had its center in the South. But as the Negro people spread to the north, east and west seeking to escape the Southern hell, the violence, impelled in the first instance by economic motives, followed them, its cause also economic. Once most of the violence against Negroes occurred in the countryside, but that was before the Negro emigrations of the twenties and thirties. Now there is not a great American city from New York to Cleveland or Detroit, from Washington, the nation's capital, to Chicago, from Memphis to Atlanta or Birmingham, from New Orleans to Los Angeles, that is not disgraced by the wanton killing of innocent Negroes. It is no longer a sectional phenomenon.

Once the classic methods of lynching was the rope. Now it is the policeman's bullet. To many an American the police are the government, certainly its most visible representative. We submit that the evidence suggests that the killing of Negroes has become police policy in the United States and that police policy is the most practical expression of government policy.

Our evidence is admittedly incomplete. It is our hope that the United Nations will complete it. Much of the evidence, particularly of violence, was gained from the files of Negro newspapers, from the labor press, from the annual reports of Negro societies and established Negro year books.

But by far the majority of Negro murders are never recorded, never known except to the perpetrators and the bereaved survivors of the victim. Negro men and women leave their homes and are never seen alive again. Sometimes weeks later their bodies, or bodies thought to be theirs and often horribly mutilated, are found in the woods or washed up on the shore of a river or lake. This is a well-known pattern of American culture. In many sections of the country police do not even bother to record the murder of Negroes. Most white newspapers have a policy of not publishing anything concerning murders of Negroes or assaults upon them. These unrecorded deaths are the rule rather than the exception—thus our evidence, though voluminous, is scanty when compared to the actuality.

Causes Célèbres

We Negro petitioners are anxious that the General Assembly know of our tragic causes célèbres, ignored by the American white press but known nevertheless the world over, but we also wish to inform it of the virtually unknown killed almost casually, as an almost incidental aspect of institutionalized murder.

We want the General Assembly to know of Willie McGee, framed on perjured testimony and murdered in Mississippi because the Supreme Court of the United States refused even to examine vital new evidence proving his innocence. But we also want it to know of the two Negro children, James Lewis, Jr., fourteen years old, and Charles Trudell, fifteen, of Natchez, Mississippi who were electrocuted in 1947, after the Supreme Court of the United States refused to intervene.

We want the General Assembly to know of the martyred Martinsville Seven, who died in Virginia's electric chair for a rape they never committed, in a state that has never executed a white man for the that offense. But we want it to know, too, of the eight Negro prisoners who were shot down and murdered on July 11, 1947 at Brunswick, Georgia, because they refused to work in a snake-infested swamp without boots.

We shall inform the Assembly of the Trenton Six, of Paul Washington, the Daniels cousins, Jerry Newsom, Wesley Robert Wells, of Rosalee Ingram, of John Derrick, of Lieutenant Gilbert, of the Columbia, Tennessee destruction, the Freeport slaughter, the Monroe killings—all important cases in which Negroes have been framed on capital charges or have actually been killed. But we want it also to know of the typical and less known—of William Brown, Louisiana farmer, shot in the back and killed when he was out hunting on July 19, 1947 by a white game warden who casually announced his unprovoked crime by saying, "I just shot a n—r. Let his folks know." The game warden, one Charles Ventrill, was not even charged with the crime.

Typical Cases

We cite some typical cases from the voluminous evidence. Each represents a part of the pattern of genocide. This pattern repeats itself throughout the nation, south and north, rural and urban. It is a pattern of government-directed and sanctioned genocide. The following are typical of police killings:

HENRY GILBERT, 42, was beaten to death in the Harris County, Georgia jail in May, 1947. That was in the South.

But in the north, Beverly Lee, 13, was shot and killed in Detroit, Michigan on October 12, 1947 by Patrolman Louis Begin. Mrs. Francis Vonbatten, of 1839 Pine Street, Detroit, testified she saw Lee and another boy walking down the street when Begin's squad car approached. She heard an officer say "Stop, you little son-of-a-bitch," and then she heard a shot. The officer was cleared by Coroner Lloyd K. Babcock.

ROLAND T. PRICE, 20-year-old war veteran, was shot and killed in Rochester, New York, by six patrolmen who fired twenty-five bullets into his body just after he had viewed the Bill of Rights and the Declaration of Independence on the "Freedom Train." He went into a restaurant where he complained he had been short changed. Patrolman William Hamill was called, drew his gun, forced Price outside, where he was joined by five other officers. All began shooting. All were cleared.

VERSIE JOHNSON, 35, a saw mill worker of Prentiss Mississippi, was shot to death in August, 1947 after he fled when a white woman raised the cry of rape. Three white officers, members of a posse that tracked Johnson down, were arrested and charged with manslaughter. They were exonerated.

RAYMOND COUSER was shot and killed by Patrolman Frank Cacurro on Montrose Street in Philadelphia, on November 16, 1947. Eyewitnesses said they saw the patrolman with drawn revolver stalking Couser as he walked down the street, Couser apparently unaware that he was being followed. The patrolman said he thought Couser was armed and had been called to the vicinity because of a quarrel in the Couser home. Couser was not armed. The patrolman received no punishment.

CHARLES FLETCHER, also of Philadelphia, was shot and killed on November 16, 1947 by Patrolman Manus McGettingan who claimed he killed him after receiving a call about a prowler. Fletcher, who had no police record, had worked for ten years at the Exide Battery Company.

CHARLES CURRY, 23, was slain by Patrolman Nolan O. Ray, who in civilian clothes, had ordered a Negro sitting beside him to move. The Negro passengers complained and Ray jumped to his feet, drew his revolver, and ordered all Negroes "to take their hands out of their pockets." When Curry did not comply swiftly enough, Ray shot and killed him. Ray was dismissed from the force and indicted for murder.

GEORGE THOMAS, Negro youth, was shot and killed by a Kosciusko, Mississippi patrolman who claimed Thomas tried to escape after being arrested on February 2, 1948.

A Negro prisoner, on May 23, 1948 in Augusta, Georgia, was beaten to death by a prison guard when he refused to work in a snake-infested ditch.

ROY CYRIL BROOKS, of Gretna, Louisiana, was shot and killed on February 27, 1948, by Patrolman Alvin Bladsacker. Brooks was a prominent trade unionist. He was involved in an argument with a bus driver when Bladsacker pulled him off the bus and killed him.

JAMES TOLLIVER, 40, of Little Rock, Arkansas, was beaten to death in February of 1948 by Patrolman Blaylock. Tolliver was trying to help a drunken woman when Blaylock came up behind him and struck him on the head. He died almost instantly.

JOHN JOHNSON, 50, was slain by Birmingham, Alabama, police who claimed he was resisting arrest on March 29, 1948.

ALMA SHAW, 42, was slain by Birmingham police on April 27, 1948 who claimed she was resisting arrest.

MARION FRANKLIN NOBLE, 19, was slain by Birmingham police on April 27, 1948 who said he resisted arrest.

WILLIE JOHNSON was shot to death, on May 2, 1949, by two Brunswick, Georgia policemen who claimed that "he was looking at a house suspiciously." Johnson, 58, had been a resident of Brunswick for fourteen years, was a county employee and a deacon of St. Paul's Baptist Church.

ROBERT J. EVANS, 86 years old, a patriarch of Norfolk, Virginia was shot and seriously wounded on December 12, 1950 by Patrolman E. M. Morgan who said the old man assaulted him.

DANNY BRYANT, 37, of Convington, Louisiana, was shot and killed in October of 1948 by Patrolman Kinsie Jenkins after Bryant refused to remove his hat in the presence of whites.

HERMAN GLASPER, 30, was shot and killed in Bryan County, Georgia, during the week of January 2, 1949 by Corporal Dee E. Watson, Georgia State Trooper. Glasper had been arrested on suspicion of stealing a hog. Sheriff E. W. Miles said that the shooting was "an accident."

CHARLES PHIPER was shot in the back and slain in his Brooklyn, New York home by Brooklyn police on February 18, 1949. Police entered his home without a warrant and with no offence charged against Waddell. They claimed they were looking for a gambling game when they forced entry into Waddell's home. No evidence of gambling was found.

IKE CRAWFORD, a 29-year-old prisoner in the Richmond County, Georgia jail was beaten to death on June 5, 1948 by Guards David L. Turner, Horace Wingard and Alvin Jones. The men were indicted for "prison brutality." A coroner's jury, however, reported that Crawford died of a "liver disease."

Other Race Murders

Not all murders or assaults are by police. Some result from segregation, from living in fire traps, or from denying badly injured Negroes entry into hospitals because of their color. Others result from the constant declaration and determination of white supremacists that Negroes have no rights that a white man is bound to respect. The following cases are typical:

MR. AND MRS. O'DAY SHORT and their two little girls were burned to death two days before Christmas, 1945, in a fire of incendiary origin set by persons who did not want them to move into a "white" neighborhood in Fontana, California. They had received threatening notes and the police informed them they were "out of bounds." While the family was away, the house was sprayed with an inflammable chemical. When a match was lighted upon the family's return, there was an explosion and all four were fatally burned.

Three Negro children, RUBY NELL HARRIS, 4, MARY BURNSIDE, 8, and FRANKIE THURMAN, 12, of Kosciusko, Mississippi were slain on January 8, 1950 by three white men, Leon Turner, Malcolm White and Windel Whitt, who also raped PAULINE THURMAN, 17, and shot THOMAS HARRIS, father and stepfather of the children. Harris died of his wounds. Turner and Windel Whitt received life sentences. Malcolm White was sentenced to ten years imprisonment.

MATTHEW AVERY, 24, student at North Carolina A & T College died after an auto accident on December 8, 1950 when he was refused admittance to Duke Hospital at Durham. He died an hour later.

LEROY FOLEY died in Breckinridge County Hospital, Hardinsburg, Kentucky in August, 1950, after he and two other Negroes lay on the floor three hours, refused medical attention for injuries in an automobile accident. Betty Graves, a nurse in the hospital, said they were refused treatment "because we don't have facilities for colored people." A Negro ambulance service was called to transport the men out of the hospital. It was seventy miles away and did not arrive for three hours. Jesse Lawrence, its driver, said, "the blood had not even been wiped from their faces."

JESSIE JEFFERSON, of Jackson, Georgia, was slain on his farm on June 12, 1948 by two men who accused him of not moving his wagon over to the right quickly enough when they wanted to pass him.

ELLIS HUDSON, 50, of Nacogdoches, Texas, was shot and killed by a Texas constable, one Heppenstead, who had beaten and imprisoned Hudson's son during the week of March 21, 1948 because the boy did not address him as "sir." The elder Hudson was killed when he came to court to arrange bail for his son.

HOSEA W. ALLEN, of Tampa, Florida was shot and killed on September 26, 1948 when he asked to be served a bottle of beer. Victor Pinella, the proprietor of the tavern, explained that he killed Allen because he did not permit Negro customers. He was freed.

ISAIAH NIXON, 28-year-old war veteran, was shot and killed in the presence of his wife and children on September 6, 1948 after he had voted in that day's primary election in Montgomery County, Georgia. A jury freed M. L. Johnson, the killer.

WILLIE PALMER, was shot five times and critically wounded by J. C. Bradford on June 24, 1950, because he sat in the white section of a restaurant operated at the Knox Glass Company in Jackson, Mississippi. Sheriff Troy Mashburn said the shooting was in "self-defense."

ROBERT MALLARD, 37-year-old Negro salesman, was shot and killed in Lyons, Georgia, on the night of November 20, 1948, after he had led a campaign defending the right of Negroes to vote. His car was stopped and ambushed by three cars set up as a road block. He was killed in the presence of his wife, Mrs. Amy Mallard, his child, and two cousins. Mallard had been warned not to vote in the Democratic primary election.

OTIS NEWSOM, of Wilson, North Carolina, 25-year-old war veteran and the father of three children, was shot and killed during the week of April 4, 1948 by N. C. Strickland, gas station operator. Strickland killed Newsom after the Negro asked that he service his car with brake fluid he had just purchased.

ROE NATHAN ROBERTS, 23-year-old war veteran, was shot and killed in Sardis, Georgia, when he failed to say "yes sir," to a white man in May of 1947.

ONE WELL-KNOWN genocidal organization in American history is the Ku Klux Klan. One noted Klan leader in the early 20th century was Richard Loomis." We don't want anybody to join," he said, "who's not ready to get out and kill n—rs and kill Jews." Two days later, at a meeting at 198½ Whitehall Street, Atlanta, Loomis said, "There is no end to what we can do through the ballot. If we want to bury all n—rs in the sand, if we will organize white Gentiles politically to combat the Jew and n—r blocs, we can pass laws enabling us to bury all n—rs in the sand." During the same year, Loomis told the Imperial Kloncilium of the Ku Klux Klan, East Point Klavern, Georgia, "We propose that all n—rs in America be shipped back to Africa with timebombs on board the ship as an economy measure."

Other racist terrorist organizations include, as we shall show, the American Gentile Army, sometimes called the Commoner Party, and J. B. Stoner's Anti-Jewish Party. But by far the largest is the Ku Klux Klan, chartered in most of the Southern states as well as elsewhere. Its philosophy, so reminiscent of Hitler's, is exemplified by the statement of its Imperial Wizard, Hiram W. Evans, writing in "Negro Suffrage—Its False Theory":

"The first essential to the success of any nation, and particularly of any democracy, is a national unity of mind. Its citizens must be One People (Ein Volk). They must have common instincts and racial and national purpose. . . . We should see in the Negro race a race even more diverse from ourselves than are the Chinese, with inferiority . . . applies equally to all alien races and justifies our attitude toward Chinese, Japanese, and Hindus. . . . No amount of education can ever make a white man out of a man of any other color. It is a law on this earth that races can never exist together in complete peace and friendship and certainly never in a state of equality."

Operating on this principle thousands of hooded, masked Klansmen, robed in white, ride through the countryside, killing, flogging, shooting, wrecking, pillaging. Their activities are winked at by what passes for democratically elected legal authority, when not initiated by it. Police officers themselves often participate in their activities. The target of their organized terror is almost always the Negro people—although with increasing frequency members of the Klan are hired to prevent the unionization of workers to keep wages down. The terror organized by the Klan, with the cooperation as we shall prove, of the various states, is a powerful mechanism in preventing almost two-thirds of those eligible to vote under the law and the Constitution in seven Southern states from actually voting. It is the major instrument of terror in preventing political democracy in Southern United States, thus perpetuating in power, as we shall show, a minority clique and the corporate interests they represent, not only locally but also nationally in the Federal Congress.

Mental Harm

Our evidence includes many instances of psychological terror and mass intimidation on the basis of "race" particularly as perpetrated by the Klan. These, we maintain, contravene that part of the Genocide Convention forbidding the causing of "serious mental harm to members of the group." Some indication of this terror is manifest in the following cases:

Cyclops Roper of the Georgia Ku Klux Klan reported on April 1, 1946 that he had conferred with gubernatorial candidate Eugene Talmadge on ways and means of keeping Georgia Negroes from voting and that Talmadge had replied by writing the word "Pistols" on a scrap of paper.

In a radio address from Jackson, Mississippi, on June 22, 1946, Senator Theodore Bilbo of that State announced that he was a Klansman, he called upon "every red-blooded American in Mississippi to resort to any means at their command" to prevent Negroes from voting. After a good deal of violence against those Negroes who tried to vote, Bilbo was re-elected.

On March 2, 1948, 300 robed Klansman at Wrightsville, Georgia, paraded around the courthouse square and burned a cross there on election eve. Said Dragon Green: "Whenever the Negro takes his place at the side of the white man blood will flow in the streets of the South."

On March 20, 1948, at Jeffersonville, Georgia, crosses were burned on the courthouse lawn on Saturday and Sunday nights before the county primary day. Small coffins labeled "KKK" were placed on the doorsteps of those Negroes who it was thought might try to vote.

At Columbus, Georgia, KKK white supremacy leaflets were dropped from an airplane over Negro districts just before the primary selection.

On June 30, 1948 at Macon, Georgia, a cross was burned before the home of Larkin Marshall, Negro Progressive Party candidate for the United States Senate. He also received notes threatening him if he did not withdraw his candidacy.

On July 23, 1948 at Stone Mountain, Georgia, three thousand robed Klansmen, convening in cars from all parts of Georgia and fourteen other states, inducted seven hundred new members under a 30-foot fiery cross. Herman Talmadge was extolled by Dragon Green as "the only man in the gubernatorial race who believed in white supremacy." Green again predicted that blood would flow in the streets if Negroes were given their Constitutional rights.

On August 9, 1948, on the eve of the Democratic primary at Columbia, South Carolina, the Klan burned fiery crosses in front of a Negro church where the mechanics of voting were being explained.

At Nashville, Tennessee, postal authorities on November 2, 1948 began an investigation of hundreds of threatening notes received by Negroes and signed by the Klan warning them not to vote.

In Florida on November 3, 1948 a Klan motorcade burned fiery crosses in Negro residential districts from Mount Dora to Miami.

A Klan procession, including fifty motor cars, paraded through the streets of Brighton, Alabama, on December 22, 1948, to intimidate Negroes.

A similar demonstration for the benefit of the Negro people took place on the same date in Bessemer, Alabama.

Forty automobiles filled with hooded Klansmen warned the student body of Talladega College in Alabama on January 17, 1949 not to participate in the Alabama Students Conference on Civil Rights.

Mrs. J. M. Sweat, a Negro school teacher, received a threatening note from the Ku Klux Klan on January 24, 1949 when she moved into a white neighborhood in Richmond, Virginia. The note contained a bullet and said, "You Are Not Smart."

Police provided an escort for a Klan demonstrated bearing an electric cross and Klan flags in Tallahassee, Florida on January 27, 1949.

At Denmark, South Carolina on February 9, 1949, 269 hooded Klansmen held an anti-Negro demonstration, parading through the rain, carrying red flares.

Klan activities, and their mob counterparts, are not confined to the South. Organized anti-Negro violence, often under police protection, has spread its pattern in the North.

At Union, New Jersey, on February 19, 1949, a five-foot cross was burned before a Negro school after a meeting protesting the death sentence against the so-called Trenton Six Negroes.

At Peekskill, New York, on August 27, 1949 a cross was burned during the assault of veterans upon those attending a concert.

This psychological and physical terror carried out by the Ku Klux Klan and other organized groups against the Negro people deters millions of them, as it is intended to from voting or otherwise exercising their rights under the Constitution of the United States and the Charter of the United Nations. Under the weight of these calculated demonstrations the Negro people, particularly in the South, live their lives in fear of violence for allegedly overstepping one of the many prohibitions in the extra-legal white supremacy code enforced by the Klan—which often operates as a "state within a state." If Negroes sometimes avoid physical violence, they never escape from "serious mental harm directed against the group," in violation of Article II of the Genocide Convention.

Denial of Right to Vote

If millions of Negroes are prevented from voting through fear, thousands are brave enough to attempt it and risk the fate of Robert Mallard, Isaiah Nixon, and Macio Snipes, tragic instances of Negroes killed in Georgia for voting in accordance with their legal right under the Constitution. Typical of the experiences suffered by Negro citizens in attempting to vote were those testified to before a Senate Investigating Committee inquiring into the election of Senator Theodore Bilbo of Mississippi in 1946. Despite such testimony as the following, the Senate Committee ruled that no terror had occurred during the election.

Etoy Fletcher, a veteran of the armed forces of the United States, testified that on July 12, 1946 when he attempted to register for voting at Brandon, Mississippi, he was beaten and flogged with a heavy wire cable. He was threatened with death, he said, if he made another attempt to vote.

Richard Daniel, a veteran of the armed forces of the United States, testified that on July 2, 1946 at Gulfport, Mississippi, he was struck on the head by two election officials when he attempted to register for voting and then he was arrested and beaten unconscious in his cell.

Dr. William Bender, a minister from Touhaloo College, Touhaloo, Mississippi, testified he had been kept from the polls on Election Day by two white men who insulted him and another white man who met him at the polls with a pistol.

Joseph Parham testified that the sheriff had told him on election day, "You're too old to get in trouble" and that white men asked him, "What kind of flowers do you want?"

The Reverend C. M. Eiland, minister of Louisville, Mississippi, testified that two white men stopped him at the polls and told him they didn't want Negro soldiers (veterans) to vote. . . .

J. D. Collins, of Greenwood, Mississippi, testified that the Mayor of Greenwood and two other leading citizens had called on him and A. C. Montgomery, giving them a list of Negro veterans and urging them to visit them and tell them not to vote.

Witnesses testified before the Senate Committee that terror had kept all but 2500 of the state's potential 500,000 Negro voters away from the polls on Election Day. Mississippi's tactics are common to other Southern states were the Fourteenth and Fifteenth Amendments to the Constitution of the United States are honored in the breach but not in the observance. Your petitioners venture the hope that this will not be the case.

The "Black Belt"

The primary locale of the genocide being practiced against the American Negro people, both historically and geographically, is the so-called Black Belt of the southern United States, where some five million Negroes live, a third of the Negro population of the United States. The Black Belt forms a crescent through twelve Southern

states, from Virginia's tidewater into North Carolina, South Carolina, lower and central Georgia and Alabama, into Florida, engulf-
ing Mississippi and the Louisiana delta and wedging into eastern
Texas and southeast Tennessee, with its western anchor in southern Arkansas. Here the Negro population, historically a majority, is
larger than the total population of such countries as Switzerland or
Norway.

Because this area was the core of chattel slavery, at least legally
abolished some eighty-six years past, and because it has the greatest
concentration of the plantation system of sharecropping and peonage, those remnants of slavery, the Black Belt is the chief source
of the racist contamination that has spread throughout the United
States. Here the American citizen who is a Negro is virtually without political or economic rights of any kind. He is bound to the soil
by a system of virtual peonage and unending debt. He is paid for
the most part, not in wages but by a portion of the crop he raises.
The constant threat of violence prevents him from asking an
accounting from the landlord when, as is often the case, at the end
of the season he is told no money is due him. Many black men have
been killed for demanding such an accounting.

Most sharecroppers work from dawn to dark for a living which
verges on starvation. Often these black Americans are not even able
to quit or move not only because of lack of money but because of
ancient debtors' laws which make it a crime to move while owing
money, a condition that is constant for sharecroppers forced to buy
at extortionate prices on credit in plantation stores. Much of the
law of those states in the Black Belt, moreover, is directed towards
guaranteeing an American peasantry without political or human
rights available to work the land without pay sufficient for proper
livelihood.

The Problem Agrarian in Origin

"The Negro question in the United States is agrarian in origin,"
writes Harry Haywood in his authoritative *Negro Liberation*.

Haywood stated: "It [the Negro question] involves the problem
of a depressed peasantry living under a system of sharecropping,
white boss supervision, debt slavery, chronic land hunger and depen-
dency—in short the plantation system, a relic of chattel slavery.

"It presents the curious anomaly of a virtual serfdom in the very heart of the most highly industrialized country in the world. Slave-whipping barbarism at the center of 'enlightened' twentieth century capitalist culture—that is the core of America's race problem."

The South's plantation system, concealed by the United States census through listing as "farms" those tracts operated by share-croppers, is based on cotton as the chief money crop. In 1949 the crop, produced for the world market in successful competition with the "coolie" labor of Egypt and India, brought one and a half billion dollars. The growing and marketing of this crop by the comparatively few large land-owners who dominate this phase of American agriculture rest on large scale credits advanced, in the last analysis, by the country's largest banks. These banks in turn are dominated by the Morgans, Rockefellers, du Ponts, Mellons and associated financial oligarchies who dominate the South not only through command of credit for its chief money crop but through even more intimate control of the chief industries of the South. Thus, they profit not only from the exploitation of the sharecropper but from the depressed industrial wages that result from this exploitation.

Arthur F. Raper, well known authority on the American South, declares that the Black Belt plantation system is an incubus weighing on white workers as well as Negro and guaranteeing that industrial wages remain low. He writes:

"The Black Belt sketches the section of the nation where the smallest proportion of adults exercise the franchise and it defines the most solid part of the Solid South. . . . Human relations in Atlanta, Birmingham, Montgomery, Memphis, New Orleans and Dallas are determined largely by the attitudes of the people of the Black Belt plantations from which many of their inhabitants, white and Negro, came. The standard of living in these cities does not escape the influence of this area of deterioration. No real relief can come to the region so long as the planter, who wants dependent workers, can confound the situation by setting the white worker over against the black worker, and so long as the industrialist, who wants cheap labor, can achieve his end by pitting

urban labor against rural labor. There are literally millions
of farm laborers in the Black Belt who are eagerly waiting
an opportunity to work for wages even smaller than are now
being paid textile and steel workers in southern cities."

Genocide for Profit

Thus the foundation of this genocide of which we complain is economic. It is genocide for profit. The intricate superstructure of "law
and order" and extra-legal terror enforces an oppression that guar-
antees profit. This was true of that genocide, perhaps the most
bloody ever perpetrated, which for two hundred and fifty years
enforced chattel slavery upon the American Negro. Then as now it
increased in bloodiness with the militancy of the Negro people as
they struggled to achieve democracy for themselves. It was particularly bloody under slavery because the Negro people never ceased
fighting for their freedom. There were some two hundred and fifty
years of chattel slavery in the United States.

The genocide that was American slavery, the killing of part of
the group so that the remainder could more readily be exploited for
profit, resulted in two wars. The first was the aggression against
Mexico in 1846 seeking more territory for the expansion of slavery.
The second was the Nineteenth Century's deadliest, war—the Civil
War of the states. The American Civil War (1861–1865) was a revolutionary war in which the American people destroyed the slaveocracy, that minority of slaveholders who had controlled the country and its government for generation. In the wake of this conflict, a
rising industrialism, then the dominant and most revolutionary current in American life, joined with four million liberated slaves and
the poor whites of the South to impose its democracy on the former slaveocracy, giving the Negro the right to vote and to participate in the South's political life.

The War Amendments: The Historical Background

It was during this progressive period, before industry had pyra-
mided into monopoly, and in an effort to complete the revolutionary struggle, that the Fourteenth and Fifteenth Amendments to the
Constitution were passed, to assure full and unimpeded rights of
citizenship to the Negroes. The Fourteenth Amendment was ratified

on July 28, 1868, the Fifteenth on March 30, 1870. If these constitutional safeguards were enforced, instead of being effectively abrogated by administrative and legislative action and inaction—backed by perverse judicial decisions of the United States Supreme Court— it is unlikely that this petition would be necessary.

The Fourteenth Amendment provides . . . "No State shall make or enforce any law which shall abridge the privileges or immunities of citizens of the United States; nor shall any State deprive any person of life, liberty, or prosperity without due process of law; nor deny to any person within its jurisdiction the equal protection of the laws. . . ."

The Fifteenth Amendment asserts, "The right of citizens of the United States to vote shall not be denied or abridged by the United States, or by any State, on account of race, color, or previous condition of servitude." It adds that "The Congress shall have power to enforce this article by appropriate legislation." The Federal Government's chief legal arm, the Department of Justice, hold that Congress has passed no enabling legislation permitting it to move for the enforcement of these laws, Theron Lamar Caudle, Assistant Attorney General and head of its Criminal Division of the Department of Justice, explicitly declaring in 1946 that "the federal government is powerless."[1]

For a short time the Federal Government under the Republican Party gave force to these Amendments. Democracy flourished. A free public school system was established for the first time in the South. Thousands of Negroes joined with democratic white officials to govern and administer states, cities, and counties, serving as legislators, mayors, tax assessors, members of school boards, and peace officers. Twenty-three Negroes were elected by the Southern people to the United States Senate and the House of Representatives, thirteen of them being former slaves. All remnant of slavery, all forms of segregation and discrimination were abolished by laws which for a short time were enforced.

The Republican Party, however, then the nation's dominant party and the instrument of a Northern industry fast becoming

---

[1] *An Appeal to the World,* National Association for the Advancement of Colored People, New York, 1947, p. 40.

trustified, deserted the Negro•people in 1876. They made a political "deal" with Southern Democrats which made the Republican, [Rutherford B.] Hayes, president in return for giving a free hand in the South to the former slaveholders. This political deal merely formalized the alliance of Northern industry and Southern Bourbons to put down the growing resistance of labor and the farmer to the grasping power and wealth of monopoly. Southern Bourbons were obviously safer allies for defending the *status quo* than the progressive Negro–white alliance in the South.

The Negro people fought back chiefly through the Populist parties that opposed the Wall Street trusts through the eighties and nineties of the last century. But their fight became more hopeless against the increased power of American monopoly. Terror was unleashed against them at home—there were 1,955 *recorded* lynchings from 1889 through 1901, according to the minimal count of Tuskegee Institute. Side by side went terror unleashed abroad, as American imperialism entered the international arena by subjugating the Filipino, Puerto Rican and Cuban people and reduced many Latin-American countries to economic and political vassalage.

The Growth of Terror

It was during this period of American imperialist adventure abroad that most of the state laws segregating Negroes and illegally denying them the vote were enacted in the Southern states. Disfranchisement laws were passed in Louisiana in 1898, in North Carolina and Alabama in 1901, Virginia, 1902, Georgia, 1908, Oklahoma, 1910. They but codified what was taking place in life. They disfranchised poor whites as well as Negroes, thus breaking the Populist movement. It was during this period, too, in which Negroes still had a remnant of political power, that the spurious charge of rape was elevated into an institution, an extralegal political instrument for terrorizing all Negroes, particularly those demanding their rights under the Constitution. With the charge of rape, reaction sought to justify its bestiality and to divorce from the Negroes those white allies who had helped to carry out the democratic practices of Reconstruction.

In November, 1898, during the Spanish-American War, Colonel A. M. Wadell said in North Carolina, according to the Raleigh *News & Observer* that "we are resolved" to win the elections in

Wilmington, North Carolina, "if we have to choke the current of Cape Fear with carcasses. The time for smooth words has gone by; the extremist limit of forbearance has been reached." Five days later the Colonel led an armed force against the Negro–white administration of Wilmington, slaughtered scores, and announced himself the new mayor. The Government gave silent assent.

In 1900, when both men and newspapers spoke less circuitously than they do today, the San Francisco *Argonaut* said: "We do not want the Filipinos. We want the Philippines. The islands are enormously rich, but, unfortunately they are infested by Filipinos. There are many millions there and it is to be feared their extinction will be slow." In the same vein and in the same year Senator [Benjamin] Tillman of South Carolina took the floor of the United States Senate and announced: "We took the government away. We stuffed ballot boxes. We shot Negroes! We are not ashamed of it!"

Genocide and War

Thus there is ample historical precedent for genocidal crime increasing against the Negro people in time of war or threat of war as it is now increasing and has been since 1945. As Senator Edwin C. Johnson remarked on May 17, 1951 in the United States Senate, calling for an end of the Korean War, that conflict is "a breeder of bitter racial hatred." Murder on the basis of race by police and courts, as in the typical cases of the innocent Willie McGee in Mississippi and the Martinsville Seven in Virginia, has long since become so frequent and widespread as to constitute an American phenomenon. Now it is increasing.

It is increasing partly because unpopular war requires a silencing of the people, a breaking of their will for resistance. Increasing violence against the Negro people goes hand in hand with increased repression throughout American life. The passive conformity found in American universities, where any new or democratic idea is suspect, according to the *New York Times*, is but a part of this larger pattern. Reaction knows that liberty is indivisible; that a victory for the Negro people in their fight for freedom may well presage a victory for labor and the forces of peace. Moreover, it feels that clamor against this baleful American crime, against genocide by the Government of the United States, is unendurable when all iniquity is supposed to rest with the enemy. The very presence of the Negro people in the United States under the existing circumstances is an indictment and an exposure that evokes hatred against them.

In addition, the great majority of Negroes are for peace, and peace endangers profits. George Bott, general counsel for the National Labor Relations Board, has formally ruled that advocacy of peace by a worker is cause for discharge. The venerable Dr. W.E.B. Du Bois, elder statesman of the Negro people, man of letters and scholar of international renown, has been indicted by the Government of the United States for his advocacy of peace. Such advocacy, it is charged, makes him a "foreign agent." Paul Robeson, a spokesman for the American Negro people who is known and honored the world around, has been denied a passport for travel abroad because he speaks uncompromisingly for peace. His voice, too, endangers the profits from war. All these factors combine to make the Negro people in the United States the increasing target of reaction's genocidal fury.

The End of Genocide Means Peace

This genocide of which your petitioners complain serves now, as it has in previous forms in the past, specific political and economic aims. Once its goal was the subjugation of American Negroes for the profits of chattel slavery. Now its aim is the splitting and emasculation of mass movements for peace and democracy, so that reaction may perpetuate its control and continue receiving the highest profits in the entire history of man. That purpose menaces the peace of the world as well as the life and welfare of the Negro people whose condition violates every aspect of the United Nation's stated goal—the preservation "of peaceful and friendly relations among nations" by the promotion of "respect for human rights and fundamental freedoms for all without distinction as to race. . . ."

Our case is strong because it is true. As it cannot be effectively denied that mortals dies, so it cannot be convincingly said that Negroes in the United States are not persecuted, segregated, assaulted and killed, day in and day out, on the basis of race and in such numbers as to make this oppression an American institution. Therefore, we solemnly ask the General Assembly to condemn this genocide on the score that it is not only an international crime in violation of the United Nations Charter and the Genocide Convention but that it is a threat to the peace of the world.

The end of genocide against the Negro people of the United States will mean returning this country to its people. It will mean a new growth of popular democracy and the forces of peace. It will mean an end to the threat of atomic war. It will mean peace for the world and all mankind.

Claudia Jones

Claudia Jones (1915–1964) was a protean radical historical figure who should be remembered as a Black Nationalist, a political activist, a radical journalist, and an important American Communist. Historical opinion is coming around to the point of view that Jones is at least important as her friend Elizabeth Gurley Flynn in the history of American radicalism.

Born in the West Indies (Trinidad), Jones moved to New York City as a child, where she suffered a uniquely American poverty and oppression that only an African American woman can understand. She used her native intelligence and highly developed social conscience to articulate a response to this state of affairs.

■ ■ ■

The Struggle for Peace in the United States (1952)

Excerpt from Carole Boyce Davies, ed., *Claudia Jones—Beyond Containment: Autobiography, Poetry, Essays* (Banbury, UK: Ayebia Clarke, 2011).

President Truman, in his capacity as chief political servitor of US imperialism, once again proposed, in his recent State of the Union Message to Congress, a criminal crusade of force and violence

against the vast majority of the human race. Truman, though dema-
gogically prattling on about peace, glorified Wall Street's aggressive
expansionism which is now flagrantly directed against the colored
peoples of Asia and Africa and proposed an unrestrained armaments race.

Mr. Truman cynically boasted of the colossal size of US imperialism's armed strength, and its pile of A-bombs. By way of perspective for peace, he urged even more intensive arming to be accompanied by further cuts in consumer goods output and in real wages.
While he lectured the people about the need for "sacrifice," in a
year marked by the largest total profits in the history of American
capitalism, he proposed an additional five billion in new taxes.

Truman used hundreds of words in an effort to justify further
burdens upon the people, but not a mumbling word did he voice
about the terrible repression of civil rights in our country, the political persecution, led by his Administration, of Communist and
other working class leaders. The genocidal oppression of the Negro
people, as highlighted just before his Message by the killing of Mr.
and Mrs. Harry T. Moore, was ignored and not a phrase fell from
his lips about F.E.P.C., or anti-lynching and anti-poll tax measures.
Dropped was all talk of the repeal of the Taft–Hartley Law, but
instead he indulged in a concern for a "fair" version of that slave
statute.

Nor could the farming masses derive any satisfaction from the
Truman message. A recent Federal report signed by James Patton,
President of the National Farmers Union, indicated that two million farmers (in a total of 5–6 million farms) will be forced off the
land and into industry to meet the "defense" requirements. When
one adds the already heavy drainage of farmers' sons for the armed
forces, it is clear that further impoverishment awaits the already
greatly harassed lower-income farmers.

Of course, Truman's saber-rattling Message had its "peace-
loving" interludes, confirming the accumulating peace sentiment
in our country, to which hats must be tipped in accordance with the
demands of good campaign strategy. Thus, Truman declared: ". . .
day in and day out we see a long procession of timid and fearful
men who wring their hands and cry out that we have lost the way—
that we don't know what we are doing—that we are bound to fail.

Some say that we should give up the struggle for peace and others say we should have a war and get it over with." Mr. Truman "struggles for peace" by putting aside a total of 11 per cent of his budget to meet all the needs of all social services!

In his pose as "savior" of the "American way of life," Truman invokes the divine right to impose war's "blessings" on the Korean people and on the rising national liberation movements of the colonial and dependent countries. Moreover, Truman seeks to convince the American people of the "necessity" to rally behind Wall Street on the basis of a "peril" which he dares term "internal aggression." But Truman perpetrates a gigantic and vicious hoax when he asserts that our nation is in "peril" because the Chinese people do not want Chiang Kai-shek and the Korean people do not want Syngman Rhee; because the peoples of Egypt and Iran want to control their own natural resources and because the peoples of Indo-China, Burma, Spain and Greece want a free, democratic existence. The Truman war program, unless routed, dooms our nation to endless war in which the rich become richer and the poor poorer; it consigns the nation's youth to death for the glory of Wall Street profiteers. The Truman perspective is that of looting the national wealth, of crushing the national aspirations of the freedom-seeking peoples, of extending the Korean adventure into a World War. Stripped of its demagogy, Truman's Message confirmed our Party's estimate that the war danger has heightened, albeit its defensive tone reflects the growing counter-struggle for peace of the masses of workers and the people generally. It likewise reflected growing contradictions of an inter-imperialist character as well as within the US bi-partisan war coalition, and in effect acknowledged the decisive and ever-increasing strength of the world camp of peace, democracy and Socialism.

The utter futility of the 20-month war in Korea and [Matthew] Ridgway's seven-month stalling of the truce talks have increased the sharp uneasiness of the American people, with whom the Korean war was never popular, and who have long seen it as a threat to world peace.

The startling significance of the Truman–Churchill "secret agreements" to A-bomb Manchuria and to take the war to China, to "save" South-East Asia from its own peoples with the help of hired

Chiang mercenaries, armed with American weapons, must be viewed in the light of Truman's fundamental adherence to the criminal bi-partisan war policy, ruinous to our nation and to all humanity. And it is in this light that we must view the current Senate hearings for ratification of the so-called Japanese Peace Treaty signed without the consent of the major Asian powers and without the Soviet Union, the Dulles call for "hardening" of US policy to "overthrow" the Chinese People's Republic and the new wave of incendiary war talk.

Setbacks for Wall Street in the U.N. Assembly

The recently concluded Paris U.N. Assembly meeting graphically revealed the real reason for the Truman warning to his NATO allies against "faltering" since the road is "long and hard." For there, the exceedingly shaky nature of the coalition forming the US imperial-ist bloc in the U.N. became clear and it was evident that the satellite delegates could not be held securely by the US imperialist leash of economic sanctions.

Wall Street dollars could not eliminate the justified fear that these representatives have of their impoverished and insulted peoples. Those peoples of Western Europe, Latin America, Africa, Australia, Asia and the Near and Middle East do not want any part of a war on China. This is shown by the extreme difficulty the US had in forcing a U.N. vote denouncing the Soviet Union for "violating" its 1945 treaty with the Chiang regime, on the "theory" that it is "Soviet aggression" for the Chinese people to sweep out the butcher-regime of Chiang Kai-shek and to inaugurate a self-determined, independent, and democratic People's Republic.

It is in this light that the now tempered bulldog bark of Churchill is to be understood in his speech to Commons, following his US tour. Nor was this the only moral defeat suffered by the US imperi-alist bloc at the Assembly meeting. There was, too, the vote on U.N. admission of Greece from which the entire Latin-American bloc initially abstained and not to be forgotten is the significant presen-tation of the C.R.C. [Civil Rights Congress] petition, "We Charge Genocide," by William Patterson, precisely at a time when the Wall Street delegation was boasting of "human rights" and at a moment when the eyes of the world were on Florida, scene of the genocide bombing of Mr. and Mrs. Harry T. Moore.

New Moods for Peace

Over a year ago, Gus Hall, in his main Report to the 15th National Convention of the Communist Party, said, truly and profoundly:

> The clearer the war danger becomes, the more people move in defense of peace.

This new upsurge is based on a new appreciation of the war danger, on a growing realization that the present course of the bi-partisans has led to a dead end. It is based on a growing confidence that peace can be won. The new turn of events in Korea packed a double wallop because millions of Americans were never enthusiastic about this reckless adventure and were never sold on the idea that this was a war for which they should willingly make sacrifices. . . . We must be confident that we are going to win the working class as a class, the Negro people as a people. And that the poor farmers, church groups and large sections of the middle class are going to participate in the organized peace movement. A powerful American peace front is clearly emerging from these developments. This peace front will be based on the working class, the Negro people, poor and middle farmers and yes, sections of the capitalist class. This is especially true of the capitalist elements who see their imperialist aims best fulfilled on the "continent" and those closely tied to agriculture. (*Peace Can Be Won!* by Gus Hall, New Century Publishers, 1951).

The subsequent months have vindicated Comrade Hall's analysis. There has been and there is a maturing peace sentiment among the American people, heightened during the US imperialist deliberately-stalled Korean truce talks. A striving is evident amongst broader and broader masses for an over-all negotiated settlement of all outstanding differences among nations. Even the Gallup Poll reported seventy per cent of the American people desired a Truman–Stalin meeting devoted to resolving the US–U.S.S.R. differences. The growing peace sentiment stems not only from new sections of the population as a whole, but primarily from new sections of the working class and Negro people. More and more the inequality of "sacrifice" and the genocidal policy towards the colored peoples abroad and at home serve to expose the sickening hypocrisy in the Truman bi-partisan foreign policy. These peace moods are reflected not only in growing queries and doubts, but in an insistent note that our country take a new path—that it reverse its present bi-partisan war policy for a path of negotiation of outstanding differences between nations and for a Big Five-Power Peace Pact. This note has a real grassroots quality and is being sounded more and more frequently and openly by mothers, wives, veterans, youth and G.I.'s themselves. Despite continued and sharpened governmental harassment of the advanced defenders of peace, a "second look" is being taken as increasing masses weigh the *real* alternative to the bi-partisan dead-end—the principle of negotiation between nations, which, premised on the concept of peaceful coexistence of states with different social systems, can lead to the conclusion of a Five-Power Peace Pact.

These masses, faced by declining real wages and mounting unemployment, demonstrate a growing awareness that it is the war economy which is responsible for this suffering and are moving to challenge more boldly the monstrous bi-partisan "alternative" of an "all-out war" to "get it over with quick" or a huge armaments race and "more Koreas."

The development of these peace sentiments is not the result of a sudden awakening but rather stems from a process of long duration. Among the many forces stimulating the growth of these desires have been the 110,000 reported US battle casualties, the cynical seven-month long delay in the truce talks, the open alliance of the US rulers with Japanese and Nazi militarists and fascists; and the immense rise of the world-wide peace struggle exemplified by the liberation efforts in Asia, the Near East and Africa, the mounting hatred of US imperialism throughout Europe and the signing of the demand for a Five-Power Peace Pact by over six hundred millions of world humanity.

What is taking place is the *beginning* of a basic re-evaluation of the suicidal anti-Soviet premise of the Truman bi-partisan policy. And this applies to large masses who have not yet broken with monopoly capital's two-party system and are still attracted by the "peace" demagogy of one or another bi-partisan spokesman.

While trade-union leaders in ever increasing numbers cry out for an end to the Korean war and the anti-imperialist sentiments of the Negro people reach an all-time high level; while Truman's "holy war" propaganda is delivered a blow by the defeat of his proposal to appoint General Mark Clark as Ambassador to the Vatican; while the whole State Department effort to make peace "subversive" suffers a blow in the great victory of the acquittal of Dr. Du Bois and his associates of the Peace Information Center—at such a time Truman still waves the threat of atom-bomb superiority and projects new proposals for extending hostilities.

And Truman does not repudiate the hideous statement of his field commander in Korea, Gen. [James] Van Fleet, who felt the war in Korea was a "blessing in disguise," and that "there had to be a Korea either here or somewhere else in the world." (*New York Times,* Jan. 20, 1952.) A "blessing"—the annihilation and maiming of literally millions of men, women and children! A "blessing" which has brought the horrified condemnation of world opinion from a leading French Catholic intellectual like Charles Favril to the Women's International Democratic Federation!

US peace forces must dissociate themselves from these "blessings," not only in the interest of common decency, but also of true patriotism and internationalism. History will not excuse the American people any more than it did the German people, if we fail effectively to dissociate ourselves from our "own" racist imperialists in their drive for world conquest and domination. This makes it necessary to deepen the understanding of all peace forces of the special white chauvinist content of the Truman bi-partisan war-policy against the colored peoples of the world.

The sharpening crisis in Wall Street's foreign policy and particularly in the solidity of its bi-partisan coalition, is seen in the blunt "admissions" of failure from monopolists like Henry Ford II and Charles Wilson, accompanied by the attacks against "Truman's war" by a Senator [Robert] Taft or a Herbert Hoover.

Reflecting the crisis amongst their masters are the lamentations of such bourgeois ideologists as Demaree Bess of the *Saturday Evening Post* and Walter Lippmann. More and more, these "confessions" take the form of admitting that the danger of "Russian aggression" was a maliciously conceived Big Lie. Such expressions, causing the "free enterprise" racketeers no little worry, mainly show that the peace movement at home and abroad is making it difficult for Wall Street to *choose*, as of today, the "all-out war" alternative. It does not mean that the imperialists have lost their *urge* to war. In this connection, it is useful to refer to Comrade Hall's summary address at our Party's 15th National Convention:

> The speeches of Hoover and Taft do reflect the crisis in Wall Street's foreign policy. They are admissions of the bankruptcy of the bi-partisan war policy. They are attempts to capitalize on the growing peace sentiments of the American people. Speeches of this kind open new doors for the peace movement. But these men belong to the war camp. We can have no illusion about Herbert Hoover, Kennedy or anyone else in the war camp. (*Political Affairs*, February, 1951, p. 15.)

It would be wrong, of course, not to pay close heed to these monopolist "admissions." Some of the forces in the emerging people's coalition hold that the Left does not accurately appraise these trends and that real choice is between Hoover and Truman. Thus, I. F. Stone, starting from the correct premise that "the world can be saved by the co-existence," finds Hoover to be "much closer to Henry Wallace's old position, which was also F.D.R.'s than to Truman." "The Roosevelt–Wallace position," writes Mr. Stone, "had sufficient faith in America not to be afraid of Communism. Hoover has faith enough in capitalism to feel that Communism, as he said 'will decay of its own poisons.' *Pravda* is not afraid of the challenge but the Truman–Acheson Democrats and the Dulles–Dewey Republicans are." (N.Y. *Compass*, Feb. 5, 1952).

We agree, of course, with Mr. Stone's basic premise of the possibility of peaceful co-existence. Is this, however, as Stone holds, only a question of "faith" in one or another society? No, in part the concept is influenced by "good business" reasons of trade. But this still is not the core of the matter. The core of the matter is the mass will for peace and the people's power to impose this will on the war-makers. This must be sealed in a Five-Power Peace Pact. Then, and only then, would it be possible to conclude that the war danger had lessened. A key to Mr. Stone's error may be found in his conclusion that "the Hoover–Taft policies might easily lead in the same direction [as Truman's] if and as new Communist victories abroad frightened the propertied classes here into support of fascism."

But fear is at the heart of the present bi-partisan policy—a fear of the peoples' rule at home and abroad. History teaches that it is not the peoples' victories that lead to fascism, but their immobilization and disunity in the face of reaction's assaults. The finance capitalists move towards fascism when they become convinced that they can no longer rule in the old way: they adopt fascist methods of terror and rule rather than adhere to the most elementary democratic process at home and abroad. In resorting to this policy of external and internal aggression, they raise the hysterical cry of "aggression" against all who resist that very aggression. Thus, they howl "Soviet imperialism" and slander all movements of peoples anywhere for national liberation and national reconstruction upon democratic foundations as "internal aggression."

This policy of imperialist onslaught and fascism at home is the policy of the Truman–Dulles camp as it is of the Hoover–Taft camp. The differences between them are not of a strategic, but of a tactical, nature. Their strife is a "family quarrel" of finance-capitalist groupings, which fear and resist the peoples' victories here and abroad and some of whom, like the Mid-Western industrialists, want at this time to concentrate upon the American and Asian continents for their "spheres of interest." They are fearful of losing all in "all out" war on the European continent.

But it is a "family quarrel" which can ripen into a crisis for the entire strategy of the bi-partisan war policy. An alert peace movement can and should enter into debate on such questions, in order to strengthen their growing advantage, to press for realization of the *real* alternative—the alternative of lasting peace, based on co-existence of the U.S.A. and the U.S.S.R., on the basis of peaceful competition, honoring of commitments, negotiation of all outstanding differences and recognition of the basic democratic right of all peoples to choose their own form of government. It is this deeper ideological meaning, underlying the real concern of certain top monopolists with the "reckless pace" with which the bi-partisan camp moves to the twin disaster of war and depression, that a people's peace movement must grasp hold of, in order to curb the warmongers.

150 ■ Claudia Jones

Main New Demagogic Arguments

The real essence of US foreign policy is pro-imperialist, anti-Soviet, anti-democratic—and anti-American. This bi-partisan foreign policy seeks to destroy every "Communist State" and to annihilate every "Communist." It seeks to "overthrow internal aggression" and build "situations of strength." It poses as a "holy" crusade in order to cover its chauvinist and racist ideology as it adopts the *Mein Kampf* concept that "nationalism is the enemy of liberty."

What of the Acheson-formulated anti-Soviet "situations of strength" argument? This formula not only means continued unemployment and hastening economic crisis, but it means perpetual arming-to-the-teeth, perpetual war-mongering and forcible efforts to destroy existing governments not to the liking of US imperialism. Small wonder that the "situation of strength" policy moves the high brass to express alarm that "peace may break out" in Korea and to issue "warnings" that the flame in Korea "threatens" to end. This policy engenders, not strength, but hatred, so that the peoples of the world already compare our youth to the youth of Hitler. It is the policy of the Rommels and Mussolinis who wrote sonnets to the "beauty" of bursting shells and who gleefully watched the torture of Communists and non-Communists in concentration camps— a policy which is unfolding in the actual present building by the bi-partisans of concentration camps for "Communists first" and then for all who dare to oppose this ruinous war policy.

The more brutal "internal aggression" argument is nothing but a Truman version of the racist *Mein Kampf* aim of domination over "inferior peoples" who need the benign "blessings" of Anglo-American imperialism to lead them to "salvation." It represents a naked "white man's burden" imperialist approach of bloodily—and vainly—trying to reverse the triumphant worldwide colonial and national liberation movements highlighted by the historic victory of the People's Democratic Republic of China and inspired by the establishment of the Union of Soviet Socialist Republics.

US imperialism, faced with ever-rising and growing struggles from the oppressed Negro people within its own borders, must attempt to hide from world view its own genocidal practices, fearful lest exposure further pulverize its shibboleth of a free nation in a free world. Consequently, the fable that "nationalism is the enemy of liberty" is designed not to whittle away the concept of an arrogant boastful nation, who can "take on the world" and "get it over with quick," but in typical white supremacist manner, to heighten chauvinist nationalism and white chauvinism through the program of "imposing salvation" on "childlike" peoples to whom self-government has been ruthlessly denied in century-long suppression.

One and all, these demagogic arguments of the bi-partisans hide a policy of betrayal of the true national interests of the United States and its people. It is the Hitler dream to destroy every "Communist" state, but in the context of today it could culminate not only in world war, but in a world atomic holocaust, from which the imperialists will not and cannot emerge victorious, but in which tremendous suffering will result to our people and all the word's peace-loving peoples. What is in peril, therefore, is not the "American way of life" but the wages of workers who are asked to rob themselves of billions of dollars so that Truman and the Wall Street monopolists can roam over the earth trying to crush freedom-seeking peoples who want independence and peace and to advance socially on the basis of their choice. The peoples of the world will never yield to these Wall Street terms. The vital interests of our own country demand that a mighty peace front be built through which can emerge a people's peace coalition capable of curbing the Wall Street monopolists' drive for a Third World war and fascism. Such a peace front, based on the working class and the inherently, anti-imperialist, growing Negro people's movement, will include broad sections of the farmers and millions of people in intellectual and professional pursuits.

State of Progress towards a People's Peace Coalition

The question arises: How can we help to "build and expand" on this perspective of the people's peace coalition in the context of a day-by-day peace struggle which, in the first place, must be rooted among the workers? It must be frankly said in evaluation of the present organized peace movement in the US that the growing sentiment for peace among the workers does not yet find expression in adequate peace organization of this decisive class. Necessary for this orientation and for advancing the peace movement in the US by deepening its anti-fascist and anti-imperialist content, is rooting the peace movement among workers and organizing peace activities on union and shop levels. Any tendency to liquidate labor peace centers, under the guise of real difficulties, means only abandoning this perspective. There is no doubt that Right opportunist tendencies are camouflaged in the advocacy of such "Left" sectarian practices, while little enough is done to seek the precise forms of peace organization to which the workers do readily respond. The struggle to win the working class is fought, not in the realm of abstract theories of the Right or the "Left," but around specific issues, around policies as regards wages, speed-up equal rights for the Negro people, foreign affairs, inner union democracy, etc. In the words of Comrade Hall:

> We must have confidence that we can win the entire working class to the policies and programs based on class struggle. We can do this, not in isolation, but by organizing and leading in struggle the rank and file in the existing unions, in the departments, shops, locals and Internationals. (*Political Affairs*, December, 1949, p. 27.)

Every index shows an increasingly anti-war feeling among the workers. More and more trade-union expressions as those emanating from figures like Carl Stellato, William R. Hood, Frank Rosenblum, etc., call for a Five-Power Peace Pact. Clearly, this higher anti-war militancy of the workers emphasizes the interlocking of the fight for peace with the fight for a decent standard of living, unshackled unionism, collective bargaining, and an end to discrimination and other elementary demands. Numerous shop stewards' peace conferences and peace ballot campaigns confirm the ready response to the peace issue among the workers. Growing mass unemployment and high taxes are undoubtedly the reason for the gloomy complaints even of Social-Democratic leaders like Walter Reuther.

What bothers class collaborationist labor leaders like Reuther, of course, is the growing rank-and-file pressure of the auto workers who face mass unemployment, who are questioning the bi-partisan foreign policy which has brought them, not the promised prosperity, but worsening economic conditions. The workers see wages frozen, higher prices and taxes and the growth of repression against the people's liberties, heightened chauvinist oppression of the Negro people and enhanced corruption in government. Even Reuther's complaints can serve to tear the mask from the eyes of many workers, who may well wonder why Reuther and the class collaborationist labor leaders persist in trying to hold the workers within the framework of the two rotten old parties of capitalism.

IN THIS CONNECTION it is useful to refer once again to the advice of Gus:

> It was in Korea that the masses saw the greatest danger of a world war and a war with China. The Republicans very cleverly identified the Truman Administration with this central danger point and thus were able to capitalize on the peace feelings of the masses. We must conclude that, yes, large sections were misled. But they are for peace. They will follow the correct road in the struggle for peace if they get the right leadership. We must be able to offer the masses a practical alternative; one, which they see provides a real chance to win outside the two old parties. This alternative must correspond to this present level of understanding in the arena of political action. . . . Large sections of the working class are beginning to draw some very important lessons from the last election campaign. The big lesson is not that the trade-union leaders took a licking. The lesson is that there must be some road that does not lead into the blind alley to which the workers have been brought by the labor officialdom. This is the outlook on which we must build and which we must help to expand. (*Peace Can Be Won!* p. 54.)

The Present Organized Peace Centers

A basic ideological weakness underlies the tendency of failing to concentrate the peace struggles and organization among the workers and the Negro people. How is this to be observed in practice? Here is an actual example: An organized peace coalition exists in a particular city. This coalition in its present state experiences difficulty in getting a hall for a certain project. A fight is carried through unsuccessfully—and privately. Certain advanced forces in the coalition suggest that the peace issue is so urgent and the need so great that "broader forces" be sought out for this project. So far so good. Even the "private" negotiation, which should be criticized, is not the main point. Broader forces *are* secured and the existing peace coalition, which supports parallel peace actions, supports this one. Lo and behold! However, there are certain forces in the coalition who do not understand the Negro question, or the decisive role of the working class. Where is the emphasis of the Left forces in the coalition? They rightly express concern that this state of affairs jeopardizes the new coalition which is emerging and some of the forces in it. They themselves certainly appreciate that not all the components of the coalition will fully understand all these questions, but it is expected that they will come into the coalition on the basis of its minimum program. But its minimum program is premised on the fact that there is a great ferment for peace especially among the masses of workers and the Negro people; it is premised on the fight for labor's rights and on the effects of the war drive on the Negro people. Do the Left-progressives battle on these issues? Yes, they battle, but unfortunately ofttimes incorrectly. They usually "battle" by arguing that to struggle ideologically on these issues would "create a problem." What they fail to recognize and ofttimes fail to examine their own weaknesses which, having their source in Right opportunism and "Left" sectarianism, usually boil down to a retreat in meeting these arguments. Experience confirms, however, that many of these broader forces respond to and learn from a struggle for the correct ideological and practical position on these questions.

Errors such as this isolate the peace coalition from decisive working class forces and the Negro people. Now, no section of a united front coalition can be ignored or "asked" to accept second-class citizenship status. How much more serious this becomes when it affects the decisive core of the coalition, the labor-Negro people's alliance! Of course, where the Negro people are concerned, this reflects white chauvinism as well. Yet serious strains, affecting relations with top labor and Negro peace leaders, having a mass base on national and state levels, exist because of this most costly error in peace activity.

A key reason for such serious errors lies in the lack of a common estimate of the character and role of the present organized peace centers among labor, woman, youth and in overall peace coordination. To be concrete: can it be said that full clarity exists among progressive forces, including Communists, relative to the programmatic character of the American Peace Crusade, the American Women for Peace, the National Labor Conference for Peace, the Youth Division of the Peace Crusade? No, it cannot! The American Peace Crusade and the above-mentioned independent organized peace centers, themselves coalitions, emerged as a result of the need for an organized peace center, of a special kind, shown particularly in the powerful, grass-roots response evoked by the Stockholm Peace Petition campaign. This response came from leading forces among intellectuals and professionals, as well as among the working class and the Negro people. Thus, the American Peace Crusade [A.P.C.] came into being and dedicated itself to advancing a principled program. Key elements of the A.P.C. program are the principle of peaceful co-existence and the negotiation of outstanding differences between the Big Five Powers. The program, based also on a recognition of the war drive's ravaging effects on the working class and the Negro people, spurs the struggle for Negro-white unity. This peace coalition includes Left-progressive forces and in line with its principled advocacy of peace, programmatically rejects Red baiting and all other divisive ideologies.

Many of the forces in the A.P.C.—and in varying degrees the other peace center—express unclarities, and disagreement, on several phases of basic policy, including the whole question of the working class and its relation to the peace coalition, the role of the Soviet Union, etc. This is as we should expect in a genuinely united front peace coalition.

But a grave persistent weakness is the lack of a working class base and real roots among the Negro people. The point is not only that these weaknesses exist, but that many of the advanced Left-progressive forces fail to accept their special ideological role and, on numerous issues, in and out of the present organized peace coalitions, this weakness seriously jeopardizes the continued growth of the coalition. Consequently, entirely too much time is consumed in necessarily resolving these problems, on top levels, while the task of rooting and organizing a united front working class base goes by the board.

Experience teaches that where these questions have been
frankly subjected to friendly discussion, the progressive forces in
the coalition, together with the Left-progressives, resolve the matter
satisfactorily.

All peace forces and Left-progressives in particular, must be
keen to cooperate with every progressive tendency that may manifest
itself, under the strong pressure of the masses, in the trade-union
leadership—on *all* levels—and within the Negro people's movement. All peace forces must learn to cultivate such trends and utilize them for the building of a broad peace coalition.

This is all the more decisive, since the new and increasing difficulties of the warmongers do not imply the cessation or necessarily a lessening of the war danger. On the contrary, the masses must
be alerted as never before to combat the machinations of the war
incendiaries.

The task demands mastery of the united front and the bold
grappling with special ideological questions on all issues confront-
ing the peace movement. Some Left-progressive forces, including
some Communists, argue that the present coalition peace centers
are "too Left." "We must build broader ones and scrap the old,"
they say. Frequently this argument hides a tendency of capitulation
to so-called "broad forces" which, in fact, reject the peace coalition's minimum program. Others demonstrate in practice that to
fail to build and expand present organized peace centers is to fail to
take advantage of the current mass peace upsurge. Thus, the development of the "broader centers" is wrongly counter posed to the
strengthening of the present organized peace centers. Some Left-
progressives, including some Communists, even take the initiative
in dissuading groups who come into activity as a result of the stim-
ulus of these peace centers, from coming closer to them, in day-to-
day working relationship.

The "great debate" goes on and on, while at a standstill is the
heart and core of the real issue, that of not only moving with the
stream, but of building and consolidating united front peace organizations among the workers and the Negro people and of organizing united front activity from below on the key peace issue and
primarily on the economic and social consequences of the war
drive.

The Right opportunist danger, reflected in a neglect to come to grips with basic ideological problems relative to the peace struggle, is mainly expressed in the failure of many Left-progressives, including some Communists, to play their special ideological role of convincing people of the correctness of the previously agreed on minimum program. Nor should Left-progressives fail to note the effect that such wrong approaches have on non-Left Negro and white forces in the coalition who see their own roles being reduced and who quite correctly resent being "written off." No argument that such discussions will isolate "broader forces" holds water. The existence of an organized peace center, or even of parallel peace movements on special issues, does not excuse lack of ideological struggle in *all* coalition peace movements.

Conversely, the "Left" sectarian danger reflects a narrow approach to the peace movement and is based on a defeatist attitude that world war really is inevitable.

The necessity for broader forms of peace struggle complements, it does not contradict, the necessity of strengthening the present organized peace centers, particularly in terms of developing their working class base. To pose these efforts as mutually exclusive is to endanger not only existing organized peace centers, but the whole concept of the united front, of an anti-fascist, anti-imperialist people's peace coalition based on the working class and Negro people.

Just as there is no contradiction between a mass united front coalition policy and the special responsibilities of the Left-progressives in the fight against white chauvinism, so is there no contradiction between the development of broader movements around specific peace issues and the building and strengthening of the existing organized peace centers based on the working class and the deepening of this ideological leadership.

The Negro People and the Fight for Peace and Freedom

If it is true that the Truman war crusade, brutally exemplified in the atrocious war against the colored peoples of Asia, develops in an atmosphere of raising counter-struggle by the Negro people is developing as they resist the Wall Street bi-partisan attempt to destroy their liberation movement and their leaders—Paul Robeson, W.E.B. Du Bois, William L. Patterson, Benjamin J. Davis,

Henry Winston, James Jackson, Ben Careathers, Pettis Perry, Roosevelt Ward, Mrs. Charlotta Bass and many, many others.

But against this white supremacist, chauvinist war drive upon the peace-loving peoples of the earth, there also develops in our epoch, the liberation movement of the peoples in colonial and dependent countries. It is clear, then, that this liberation movement "is inseparably connected with the movement for peace. Therefore any forcible attempts by the imperialists to keep these peoples in a state of dependence and colonial subjection is a threat to the cause of peace." (I. A. Seleznev, in *Political Affairs,* December, 1951.)

Faced with rising anti-imperialist counter-struggle of the colonial peoples and nations and at home with the growing, and ever-more conscious anti-imperialist Negro liberation movement, American imperialism multiplies its hourly crimes against the Negro people.

At the same time there is taking place a sharpening in the whole Negro liberation movement and a dissociation from the Truman bi-partisan war policy by increasing sections of the Negro people as expressed by more and more Negro spokesmen. Thus, many State Department Negro spokesmen are competing widely in the Negro press in "warnings" to Truman that his Point Four Program, which accompanies Wall Street's imposed "blessings," is being rejected by the independence-minded peoples of Asia, Latin America, the West Indies and Africa. Thus, it is not only the forthright Dr. Mordecai Johnson, president of Howard University, who raises this issue, but even the State Department representative, Dr. Dailey, on return from a tour of the Far East and Africa, "warns" US imperialism to reject this anti-national liberation path. Further, Negro spokesmen such as P. L. Prattis, editor of the *Pittsburgh Courier,* Dr. Benjamin Mays and numerous Negro journalists, commenting on recent Truman messages, warned that "Negro voters still have to be convinced." In the words of the influential Negro historian and publicist, J. A. Rogers:

> Colored voters are convinced that they have been ruthlessly carried for a ride and exploited on the civil rights appeal. Now they are face to face with the cold facts that not a single civil rights measure has been passed in Congress. They also know that these measures have been checked on all turns by the Southern Democratic bloc. President Truman

admitted in his recent State of the Union message that these issues had not been effected. (*N.Y. Amsterdam News,* February 2, 1952.)

Nothing so points up the basic *new* element in the relationship between the struggle for peace and the Negro liberation and people's movements than this increasingly sharp criticism by the Negro people of the Truman bi-partisan policy. The Negro people as a whole see the struggle for their rights impaled on the blade of Wall Street's greed, in a war against the colored peoples of Korea which threatens to spread into a war against the oppressed colored people of the entire world.

As decisively placed by Comrade Benjamin J. Davis in his Report to the Party's Fifteenth National Convention: "The new element in the relationship between the struggle for peace and for Negro liberation is the growing acuteness of the contradiction between American imperialism in its war program, on the one hand and on the other, the struggle of the Negro people and their supporters to defend their elementary liberties and to advance the cause of full citizenship. This is by far the most important single new factor to be noted in connection with the struggle for national liberation of the Negro people."

It is exactly the "new element" basically analyzed in Comrade Davis' Report that must yet be grasped by Left-progressive forces and the Party cadres. The further significance of this fundamental relationship between the struggle for peace and for freedom was documented and analyzed by Comrade Pettis Perry. These profound contributions require study and mastery by all Left-progressives and Party cadres without delay.

An appreciation of the great contributions of Comrades Davis and Perry will do much to heighten the ideological level in the struggle against white chauvinism, which still plagues the whole peace movement. We cannot speak of the new militant features of the Negro people's movement without recognizing that this very fact places new and tremendous responsibilities on our ideological and practical work. We must sharpen the understanding of the national question, particularly as this applies to the Negro people, in order to advance the leading role of the workers in the Negro-liberation movement. This is of basic importance in the specific context of the struggle for peace in order to guarantee strengthening the alliance of the working class and Negro people. Such an alliance must form the solid core of the emerging people's peace coalition, which will reverse the present ruinous direction the imperialists are traveling.

We must put an end to the false conception that "broader forces" cannot understand the Negro question. While it would be incorrect to demand that the full program of the Negro liberation movement be part of the program of struggle of the existing organized peace movement, it is necessary to demand—and certainly to expect of Left-progressives and Communists in the peace movement—an all-out battle against the white chauvinist poison which permeates many of these movements. To assert the impossibility of spreading an understanding of the Negro question is to excuse inactivity in the fight against white chauvinism and to insult the broad masses eager for peace and democracy. We *must* convince our allies in the anti-war struggle of the correctness of the minimum program in terms of the rights of the Negro people and Negro-white unity, which they are duty bound to fight for. The struggle for peace requires a struggle against colonialism and rejection of racist warmongering. We must labor to deepen the understanding of the masses as regards the inherent relationship between the attacks on the Negro people and the attacks on the peace movement and democratic liberties, as regards the synthesis between the fight against a robber war in Asia and the imperialist attempt to thwart the Negro liberation movement and keep its leaders from exposing US imperialist claims that it is a "free nation" in a "free world."

The superb people's victories in the Du Bois case, in Stuyvesant Town and in the development of the National Negro Labor Council Movement, fused with past struggles around Trenton, Martinsville, McGee, etc., show how the struggle for Negro rights and Negro–white unity advances and heightens political consciousness on the part of participating Negro and white masses.

Merely to master the full significance of the State Department's "reason" for the denial of a passport to Paul Robeson on the grounds that "racial discrimination" is a "family matter" the public exposure of which is inimical to the interests of the security of the United States Government, is to pose the question: Why have not the peace forces fully mounted a mass campaign that can lead to victory around this prime issue involving the revered people's artist and world peace leader—Paul Robeson? All over the world, especially among the hundreds of millions of darker peoples in Asia, Africa, Latin America and the West Indies, the US imperialists are finding the Jim Crow system in this country a most serious obstacle in their path of aggression. And it is the Communists everywhere who, together with the Left-progressives, are the leaders of the masses in this sharp condemnation of the Jim Crow outrage in the United States.

Hence, ideological struggle on this front assumes urgent significance, particularly in view of the leadership assumed in all peace centers by outstanding Negro men and women. Their contributions cannot and should not be concentrated on "doing battle" on these issues. Their white co-workers must assume greater responsibility and initiative in this regard, not only because this is proper in the struggle for Negro rights, but also in order that these capable Negro men, women and youth fighters may be freed to give fullest leadership, in their authoritative positions, to building a broad peace base among the Negro people; to developing relationships with the emerging peace expressions from very broad sections of the Negro and white forces, coming from churches, fraternal organizations, Negro women's organizations, etc.

This is of prime importance, since as things are today there persists a serious lack of an organized peace movement and organization in the decisive Negro communities, particularly in the South. This lack exists in the midst of rising intensity of mass actions of the Negro people against the growing lynch murders and intimidation, as in Cairo and Cicero, Illinois, Mims and Groveland, Florida, etc.

The warmakers, trying to offset this powerful anti–Jim Crow sentiment at home and abroad, have put forward a number of prominent Negro figures to belittle and deny the existence of Negro persecution in the United States. These shameful figures include Channing Tobias, Mrs. Edith Sampson, Ray Robinson and the like. These sorry apologists for white supremacy must be exposed far more vigorously than heretofore. This can best be done by the Negro people themselves and a peace base among the Negro people on the foundation of alliance with the Negro people's movements would help greatly in exposing such misleaders. This is particularly true among Negro women, who in their significant and developing "Sojourners For Truth and Justice" movement, will have to deal with the burning problem of the war and its effects on the Negro children and the family, on Negro mothers and wives, among whom a fiercely powerful peace sentiment exists. All this will strengthen the growing mass independent women's peace movement in our country and its present independent peace center, American Women for Peace. Coming to grips with the consequences of the war effort opens up new and rewarding avenues of broad mass contact with the overwhelming majority of working class Negro women, whose militant desires for freedom and peace are the most outstanding in the nation.

Five-Power Peace Pact

The campaign for the Five-Power Peace Pact offers a magnificent opportunity to strengthen the whole organized peace movement in our country.

Barely five months old, the organized Pact campaign is receiving unprecedented response among masses who thus again show the error in hesitations on this question within the organized peace movement and among Left-progressive forces, including the Party. There is no doubt that influencing this vacillation was a certain amount of disorientation among the organized peace forces following the significant Chicago Peace Congress. Such moods as that of "hanging on hopes" that the military would effect cease-fire following the "ebbs and flows" of the truce talks, had to be quickly discarded, in the course of self-critical examination, for the plain truth that peace can only be won through mass struggle. Basically influencing the hesitancy was not only this factor but the underestimation of the decisive character of this Five-Power Pact effort which will not end until peace is assured by the signing of such a pact. Underlying all these factors, was a fundamental ideological weakness in comprehending the full implications of the possibility of peaceful co-existence between states of different social systems, in addition to a tendency to shy away from vigorous struggle, particularly among the working class and the Negro people, against vile anti-Soviet lies and fables about "Soviet imperialism."

The American Peace Crusade leadership in the Five-Power Peace Pact effort has been outstanding. It has stressed the many-sided approaches to this campaign and has served to stimulate trade-union, farm, Negro, women, cultural and youth peace forces into similar activity. Numerous A.P.C. conferences on a state level and peace workshops have been held. Many petitions carrying special appeals, such as Peace Prayers, union resolutions, etc., have been issued. Scheduled for March, in Washington, is a National Delegates Assembly involving the Crusade and many other forces who do not adhere to the entire Peace Crusade program. Here delegates from the entire country will convene to exchange experiences in the signature campaign for the Five-Power Peace Pact, with the purpose of stimulating the campaign.

Great initiative behind the Five-Power Peace Pact effort has come from the American Women for Peace which has, in many cases, boldly canvassed existing women's organizations and urged them to participate, jointly or separately, in the campaign. Supporting the work, too, is the World Youth and Friendship Book Campaign, where signatures for a Five-Power Peace Pact are gathered by young people for eventual presentation to the United Nations.

Expressions of support have come from additional varied sources, notably from trade-union leaders such as William Hood and Hugo Ernst and from many leading intellectuals, professional and cultural figures, such as Professor Anton Carlson, Dr. W.E.B. Du Bois, Dr. Robert Morss Lovett, Paul Robeson, Dr. Alice Hamilton and Professor Philip Morrison. Again, groups such as the Committee on Peaceful Alternatives and the American Friends Service Committee (Quakers) have reiterated their support of peaceful negotiations among the great powers. Significant leaders in the religious life of the country such as the Rev. Dr. Jemison, of the National (Negro) Baptist Alliance, Bishop Bromley Oxnam and Rabbi B. Benedict Glazer, have also spoken out for agreement amongst the great powers.

These, and many similar facts, not only confirm the growing pro-peace upsurge, but show that where the initiative is seized boldly, around particular issues, broader forces do come forward, unity is achieved and wider and wider segments of the population are reached.

Two forthcoming international events offer further excellent opportunities for broadening and deepening the anti-war struggle. The first is the American Inter-Continental Peace Conference, scheduled for March. The prime responsibility of US imperialism for the terrible exploitation of the peoples of the West Indies and of Central and South America, makes active participation by peace lovers of the United States in this Congress all the more significant.

In April an International Conference in Defense of Children will be held in Vienna. "To save the children, the most precious wealth of all mankind," declares the International Sponsoring Committee, "we appeal to all men and women of good will, to all organizations which are interested in the problems of children, to participate. . . . This Conference will study what can be done in order to defend the right to life, to health and education of all children in the world." Surely, profound interest of all peace forces in the United States will be manifested towards this great international event.

The Party and the Peace Struggle

The Communist Party, whose leaders are victims of Smith Act repression, can be proud of its modest contribution to the struggle for peace. What would our nation have been, had we not had the inspiring leadership of the Party led by William Z. Foster and Eugene Dennis? The whole activity of the Party has been devoted to reversing the present ruinous path of our nation, resulting from the Wall Street bi-partisan policy. The membership, in and out of the organized peace movement, have been selfless in their work for peace and have experienced and are experiencing many reprisals as the Communist Party fights for its legal rights as an American political party, a fight which is itself, of course, of the essence of the struggle against war. Communists must and do bring to the peace movement the selflessness, enthusiasm and confidence in victory characteristic of Marxists-Leninists, not because they are self-righteous, but because the Party is *correct*, because its path is the path of the development of human society.

As Communists we struggle for peace, equality, freedom and Socialism—we struggle for the best interests of the working class, the Negro people, the farming masses, the vast majority of the American people. To fulfill these high Communist principles, we must learn from the people and we must shed all moods of "spontaneity" in the peace struggle. The mastery of the united front tactic, the deepening of our ideological weapons, must be strengthened. To work to unite all people who understand that our country is in danger of war and fascism; to work so that our nation is not viewed with fear and loathing by the peoples of the world; to root our peace struggle basically among the working class and Negro people—this is the path to the achievement of the correct main line of our Party in this period. That main line seeks the emergence of an anti-fascist, anti-monopoly, people's peace coalition, that will lead to a people's front against war and fascism strong enough to curb the warmongers in 1952 and thus open to all the American people a vista of happiness, security, equality and *peace*.

Ben Davis: Fighter for Freedom

Excerpt from Claudia Jones, *Ben Davis: Fighter for Freedom* (New York: National Committee to Defend Negro Leadership, 1954).

Interracial Actions Suspect

"It is conceivable that any organization working for interracial democracy may be challenged for its campaign against race prejudice, discrimination and inequality." —NAACP Resolution on McCarthyism.

Two years ago, a cross section of prominent Negro leaders noted this trend. These leaders, in the spirit of [David] Walker's historic Appeal, issued a call to UNITE TO DEFEND NEGRO LEADERSHIP.

"Things have reached such a state in our country" their Appeal declared, "that almost any Negro leader in our country who dares to fight hard for Negro rights is headed for trouble with the law, with 'public opinion' or, with hoodlum assassins. No matter whether these leaders are Communists, non-Communists or anti-Communists, the 'explanation' is most always the same."

The 44th NAACP Convention in St. Louis strongly warned against a "discernible pattern which tends to link

advocacy of full equality for Negroes and other minorities
to subversion or un-Americanism."

This important resolution pinpointed "the atmosphere of inquisition whirling unchecked in our nation's capital until it now borders upon the proportions and destructiveness of a tornado."

Still another example of the ominous attempt to control thought
and distort truth concerning the Negro people in our country was
the US Overseas Libraries ban last year [1948] of the works of two
well-known non-Communists, Walter White and Gunnar Myrdal
(*A Rising Wind* and *An American Dilemma*).

Mr. White's book was found offensive by McCarthy because the
NAACP leader observed that *all* Negro soldiers stationed in England in late 1941, except for a single anti-aircraft group, *did only*
manual labor.

The fact that protests restored the book to the shelves does not
alter the original impulse to ban it. Even books about laughter—the
laughter of our people which hides our pain—the kind of laughter
contained in the writings of the Negro poet and writer, Langston
Hughes, *Laughing To Keep From Crying* and *Simple Speaks His Mind,*
irked McCarthy.

A crass example of witch-hunting and book-burning, which goes
by the name of Congressional "investigations" was the inquisition
attempted by McCarthy when he subpoenaed Mrs. Eslanda Goode
Robeson and sought to put on trial her two well-known books, *African Journey* and *Paul Robeson, Negro.*

But when the famous anthropologist and wife of the famed
leader, Paul Robeson, appeared, to quote a headline from the *Afro-
American,* she proved "too much for McCarthy." Among other
things Mrs. Robeson pointed out, was that her opinions and her
right to her opinions was her own business. Invoking the First and
Fifth amendments, Mrs. Robeson also called the McCarthyites'
attention to the 15th Amendment to the Constitution, declaring that
the Senate Committee headed by McCarthy, by its obvious exclusion of Negro representatives is a "very, very white committee."

This significant challenge to the McCarthyites in their very lair,
forced McCarthy to retreat!

McCarthy also banned from the US Overseas Libraries *The Races of Mankind* by Dr. Gene Weltfish, prominent white anthropologist. During the hearing when Dr. Weltfish was interrogated as a "Communist," McCarthy picked up her pamphlet and remarked: "Just opening at random I find something on page 18 of the book entitled '*The Races of Mankind*' which would interest my southern colleagues to some extent. It shows intelligence of Southern whites: Arkansas, 41:55; Northern Negroes: Ohio, *49:50.*" [My emphasis—C.J.] Yet, this *very* pamphlet was used during World War II to educate our soldiers and to destroy the Hitlerian myth of Aryan "*white supremacy.*"

Similarly, banned from the US Overseas Libraries were such works as: Doxey A. Wilkerson's "*Special Problems of Negro Education*"; Dr. W.E.B. Du Bois' "*The Souls of Black Folk*" and other works; Dr. Herbert Aptheker's "*A Documentary History of the Negro People*" and "*American Negro Slave Revolts*"; Howard Fast's "*Freedom Road*" and his other works.

Ben Davis is in jail because books *he* believes in—books which contain the science of his beliefs—known as Marxism-Leninism—are considered dangerous by McCarthy and the war makers.

This science, the science of Marxism-Leninism, explains why there is poverty and oppression in the world and how people can change all this in the process of struggle.

It shows furthermore that it is not the Communists who have created class struggle, which existed from the dawn of history, but that Communist fighters help to organize, educate, train and lead the working class to realize its life-long dream of peace, security, equality, dignity and happiness.

It is a barefaced lie that this science is a conspiracy, since its very laws and precepts hold that profound social change evolves *not* as a result of cliques, sects, or groups, but from the movement of the masses, for national independence and freedom, for security against want and poverty, for peace against war, for democracy against fascism.

The Communist Party of the U.S.A, the Party of Ben Davis, which adheres to this science, and whose ultimate program is for Socialism, is first of all the Party of the most advanced class of modern society—the working class. The plainest workers and share-croppers who suffer most under the capitalist system can quickly understand (if only they were free to hear it!) many things about it that most professors cannot understand. These workers and poor farmers and sharecroppers have a natural basis for understanding this science from their own life experiences of being dispossessed, impoverished and denied elementary necessities of life. They understand that this science is on the side of the future of mankind.

Many honest intellectuals among our people have drawn similar conclusions however, about this science which seeks to resolve the age-old battle not yet ended, between freedom and slavery, between the rights of the toiling many and the special privileges of the aristocratic few.

Dr. Mordecai Johnson, president of Howard University, more than once the target of the un-American Committee's effort to cripple this great Negro institution, in a speech at the 1941 CIO Convention, declared of Marxism-Leninism:

"At the basis of Communism there is this simple and passionate belief: that the scientific and technical intelligence which we have at our disposal in the Western World . . . in the hands of men who love the human race, could recognize the entire economic structure of the world so as to overcome the world-wide struggle for existence and build up a working population regardless of race, creed or nationality, which could feed and clothe and house its children without taking anything by violence from the human soul. . . .

"Communism has its finger on the desire of men and is saying to men all over the world, we have come at last from the ranks of those who suffer, not to make you rich, not to make you powerful, not to place you in a position where you dominate through life, but to fix it so you can sit down with your brothers of every race, creed all over this world and eat your simple bread in brotherly peace and affection."

The dynamic and principled young Methodist Negro minister, the Reverend Edward D. McGowan, chairman of the National Committee to Defend Negro Leadership, in an address to the historic meeting of the National Fraternal Council of Churches, USA,

April 30, 1953 on the theme of the defense of Negro Leadership, said:

> "...To the Negro church has been entrusted the responsibility of translating the hopes and aspirations of the Negro for dignity and freedom into reality. When my grandparents sang the spiritual, 'I Am Going to Eat at the Welcome Table One of These Days,' it is true they meant eternity. But they also meant they were looking forward to a day in time when they would no longer have to eat in the kitchens of white folks but would eat at a table of their own in their own dining room at which they would eat in freedom and with dignity."

The Rt. Rev. William J. Walls, Bishop of the African Methodist Zion Church, outspoken advocate of peace and brotherhood, himself under attack for his views, truly declared: "I do not believe these people (the McCarthyites) are afraid of ministers and Communism, they are afraid of religion and righteousness."

The sound philosophy of the late Rev. Dr. David V. Jemison of the National Baptist Convention well summarizes these thoughts: "We want for ourselves, our wives and our children everything that every other man wants for himself and his children. We do not want anything that does not belong to us as human beings."

Is this not what Negro fighters from the days of Crispus Attucks and Denmark Vesey fought and died for; is this not what the fugitive from slavery held in his heart when he eluded his captors; is this not what the mothers of our people sang through their freedom songs to us to "*Get On Board That Freedom Train*"?

This is true from Nat Turner who died on the gallows to Ben Davis who is incarcerated in a Jim Crow jail; from Frederick Douglass political refugee from the Fugitive Slave Laws to Henry Winston and James E. Jackson, Jr., political refugees from a fascism-breeding statute—the Smith Act. . . .

One of the main threats the Smith Act represents to our crusade for equal rights as Negroes in this country is that it *censors speech, thought, teaching and advocacy of social change.*

Now, as Negroes, we have got to "teach and advocate" change in the many Jim Crow laws and practices of federal, state and governmental agencies.

But the threat is: that any Negro citizen or organization advocating such changes runs the risk that some paid informer will appear in court or some government hearing to lie and testify that one's intent—*deeds and acts to the contrary*—is to "overthrow the US Government by force and violence."

The Smith Act further makes it a "criminal conspiracy" to teach or advocate or circulate almost any idea which hired stoolpigeons can testify imply "intent" to overthrow the government by force and violence, even though as in the case of Ben Davis and his co-workers—*not a single act or deed can be pointed to as showing such attempt at overthrow, simply because there aren't any.*

How then did the government "get" its "evidence"? Through stoolpigeons. One such stoolpigeon received $10,000 for his lying mess of pottage in the case of the second Smith Act trial at Foley Square. He testified to a shocked courtroom, that, if need be, he'd stool on his own mother! In cross-examination by the defense, another stoolie admitted that he recruited members of *his own family* to the Communist Party and then *turned over their names* to the FBI!

In St. Louis, Mo., the revelation that a local minister was a stoolpigeon, paid $11,000 for his services, brought almost unanimous condemnation from his congregation. His behavior was so crass that the *St. Louis American,* Negro journal, indignantly contrasted his role to that of "a partly forgotten little black minister by the name of Rev. Richard Anderson." Stressing how way back in 1854 Rev. Anderson pastored the very congregation from which this stoolpigeon came, its editorial declared that Rev. Anderson "remained in his pulpit and openly denied the forces of slavery that had the law of the period supporting them."

But nothing so exemplifies the vile role of the informer than the recent startling attempt to dislodge Dr. Ralph Bunche as a "Communist" from his high post as head of the United Nations Trustee Division. Dr. Bunche was forced to undergo the ordeal of sixteen hours of investigation before the International Employees Loyalty Board!

The case of Dr. Bunche shows to what depths justice and righteousness have sunk in this country. For on the worthless words of Manning Johnson and Leonard Patterson, two members of the growing profitable profession of *paid* government witnesses—even a man so highly placed as Dr. Bunche was not free from their infamy! Yet, for their perjury and that of Paul Crouch, a white government informer, the Department of Justice has not lifted a finger to prosecute them! Crouch even had the audacity to boast that the Department of Justice does not dare to prosecute him for perjury since to do so would mean they would have *to amnesty the jailed Communist leaders!*

An example of the worth that can be placed on Manning Johnson, for example, is his brazen admission before the Subversive Activities Control Board that he had no aversion to lying.

As observed in a brilliant column by Cliff W. Mackay, editor, *Afro-American* newspapers, ". . . in other words, as long as a lie is wrapped in the flag, it suddenly becomes no longer a lie but a sacred duty. Such is the reasoning of the man who dared point a finger at Dr. Ralph Bunche."

The man "who dared point a finger at Dr. Ralph Bunche," is the *same* Manning Johnson who testified as a government witness in the Foley Square trial of the eleven Communist leaders. If he is unworthy of belief in the case of Dr. Bunche, is he not likewise unworthy of belief in his testimony against Ben Davis, Henry Winston and their colleagues?

It was stoolpigeons of this ilk that brought "evidence" in *all* of the Smith Act trials, which "evidence" was upheld by the courts as I angrily remember, in the case of the eleven Communist leaders and that of my co-defendants in the second Smith Act trial as "*amply justified*"!

The swiftness of the retreat of the McCarthyite inquisitors in the Bunche case is significant. It indicates the widespread and growing revulsion here and abroad to the witch-hunt and the impudence with which the informers violate the Ninth Commandment: "Thou Shalt Not Bear False Witness Against Thy Neighbor."

> "*. . . Be Not Afraid*
> *Or Dismayed . . .*"
> —DAVID WALKER

More than a quarter of a century ago, this thought expressed in these calming and prophetic words in the *Appeal of David Walker,* born of a free mother, rallied thousands of Negro and white Americans to the fight against chattel slavery. The laws of that day were the Black Codes. Like the Jim Crow and thought-control laws of today—these laws, which replaced the old slave codes, also forbade the teaching of Negroes to read and write and the assembling of Negroes without permission.

A fierce attack descended on Walker's *Appeal* as well as on those who supported or even read it, from the slave and plantation owners. The secret order, of the same cloth as the Ku Klux Klan, was known as the *Knights of the Golden Circle*. The secret order outlined many prohibitions, was the main weapon on the side of the plantation and slave owners and all who challenged this order were termed "subversive" and attacked vehemently.

But Walker's call for unity of the Negro people and his words to "not be afraid or dismayed" found an echo in the hearts and minds of the Negro people and their white allies as well as among Negro leaders of both conservative and militant persuasion. It was this kind of people's unity which led to nullification and repeal of these brutal slave codes, which contravened American liberty and subverted the American dream, already sullied by chattel slavery.

Today too, our people are uniting in defense of Negro leadership.

For in addition to the question of liberty, of the fascist threat to civil rights, which I have earlier discussed, the threat of economic depression, in this richest of all lands, has already descended on our people in a more than 2-1 ratio as witness the growing unemployment lists. Like a long shadow over us, it brings in its train joblessness, starvation, eviction and the return to relief rolls, which are meager enough.

Just as there is an integral connection between the struggle against the twin danger of war and fascism and the struggle for economic security and the fate of Negro freedom, so there is a connection between that struggle and the fight for which Ben Davis and his colleagues were jailed and persecuted.

If there is anything that Ben Davis and his colleagues have been associated with and have vigorously fought for—it is for peaceful coexistence between nations and against atomic war; for a peacetime economy, for extended civil rights, for equality and democracy.

Long before it was popular to do so, Ben Davis and his Party, the Communist Party spoke out against the useless Korean War and the waste of lives of Negro and white youths. For this they were accused of being "unpatriotic" and injurious to the nation's welfare. But can anyone today hold that the Korean War—with its over 100,000 GI casualties and countless Korean dead—was other than a useless war?

It was the Party of Ben Davis that likewise exposed the Korean War as a war against the colored peoples of Asia—a war with definite racist implications, in which Negro soldiers were especially penalized.

The plain truth is that the American people in their majority ultimately opposed the criminal Korean adventure. They made it plain also they wanted no part of the Nixon–Knowland scheme to send American boys overseas to die for the profits of French colonialism in Indo-China.

It was because they fought for the goal of peace that Ben Davis and his colleagues were jailed and persecuted. *Is a minority Party, like the Communist Party, to be penalized for its scientific understanding of society—and its leaders for their clarity of vision? The truth of their views is being confirmed before the eyes of the whole world.*

The great achievement at Geneva, ending the nearly eight year "dirty war" in Indo-China, demonstrates the irrepressible will for peace of millions of the world's peoples. This peace heralds the prospect that men, women and youth strive for and believe can be won in our generation.

Were Ben Davis and his colleagues at their posts of leadership today, they would join with the great majority of people who hail this achievement. They would expose the demagogic charge of "appeasement" by those reactionaries who flail against the truce. Davis and his colleagues would join with thousands of progressive and democratic-minded people around the globe who protest new threats to world peace, such as is evidenced in the rape of the great nation of Guatemala whose democratically elected government was recently overthrown by the US–United Fruit-backed puppet, Castillo Armas. Davis and his colleagues would protest the murderous deaths of over 4,000 heroic Kikuyu people of Kenya, East Africa, for their "non-cooperation" with British imperialist perpetuated rule over their homeland and Davis and his colleagues would also oppose the US-backed efforts to remilitarize Western Germany as a threat to world peace.

The pioneering role and contributions of Ben Davis and his Party, the Communist Party, in all of these and other peace struggles, for which they were persecuted and jailed, makes it imperative, now—with the peace will of our people on the rise, with the rising anti-McCarthy movement, that Ben Davis and his colleagues should be freed to give their leadership to further successes for the people's deepest needs and aspirations. . . .

Ben Davis was not jailed for the big or little lies imputed to him and his Party, the Communist Party—Ben was jailed for ideas he does believe in.

One of the very first ideas Ben Davis and his Party believes in is that the Negro people should have full, unequivocal economic, political and social equality—not 20 years hence, not 10 years hence, but NOW! This is likewise one of the reasons why Ben and his Party support and stand ready to unite with all organizations of our people or white allies who set on this freedom goal or any aspect of this cherished goal.

Ever since Ben Davis revolted against Jim Crow conditions in his native Atlanta, against Jim Crow education, Jim Crow in the economic, political and social life of Georgia, the Wall Street rulers of our country have been trying to silence his great voice.

Yes, they hate Ben Davis.

When at one point of Ben Davis' slashing testimony in prejudiced, freedom-hating, Federal Judge Harold R. Medina's courtroom, this slick banker and owner of slums leaned over his bench to command, in insulting white supremacist fashion, of Ben Davis: "Now—be a good boy. . . ."

Ben flashed back into his teeth: "I will not be a good boy!"

Reaction has hated Ben and singled him out as a marked man from the moment he refused to "be a good boy" and accept the status quo of Negro serfdom, of lynch and mob violence in the South.

Ben Davis' own testimony best exposes the lie that it is not the Communists, but those who are continually accusing the Communists of force and violence who are themselves the real perpetrators of force and violence against the Negro people and other sections of the working class in our country.

Here is an exact excerpt of his testimony in his own words:

The Court: Mr. Davis, in these speeches that you made, did you at any time undertake to answer the charge that the Communist Party advocated the overthrow of the Government by force and violence?

The Witness: Yes, many times.

Davis (continued): I said about that, that that is just a pure Hilterian distortion of our Party in this country. I discussed this very many times and pointed out that this business of charging the Communist Party with force and violence was one of the very strangest things in the world to me. To tell me as a Negro about practicing force and violence, as a Communist, when all my life I had been hounded by this both as a Communist and as a Negro well, that just didn't make sense; and that this charge—of force and violence— usually comes from fascist sources and that it is usually uttered against the Communist Party, in order to hide the real forces of force and violence, who are the Ku Kluxers, the terrorists and the lynchers and the police brutes who attack the Negro people and who attack other sections of the working class in this country. That is the way I answered that question.

This is why they went out to get him; to silence this great tribune of American democracy, of our people, the Negro people of all the oppressed, Negro and white.

Ben Davis was born "on the other side of the tracks" in Dawson, Georgia, September 8, 1903. His grandmother was born a slave as were a couple of his aunts and uncles. His father, an editor and publisher, was a member of the Republican National Committee— whose election was greeted by burning crosses of the KKK on his front lawn. This campaign, for months of terror by the KKK against his home, hastened the early death of his mother.

When about six years of age, he attended for a few weeks a segregated "tumble-down rural school in Dawson, Georgia."

Ben also attended Summer Hill Public School, a public Elementary school in Atlanta. But because provision for public education for Negroes ended at the sixth grade in Georgia, at that time, his parents sent him to Morehouse College and then to Amherst where he "did well in studies . . . did a little debating, belonged to the glee club and orchestra, played the cornet in the band and the violin in the orchestra. And other varied campus activities."

After graduating in 1921, from Morehouse Academy, the equivalent of high school and later Amherst, where he received his Bachelor of Arts degree in 1925, Ben went to Harvard Law School and took his law degree in 1932.

After graduating from Harvard, at 28 years of age, Ben returned to Atlanta to practice law and was admitted to the Georgia Bar in 1932. Two months later came what he describes as "a turning point in my life."

Ben Davis was just starting out—with the advantage of a Harvard Law degree. He might, if he "knew his place," have achieved what success is possible for a Negro in the South and a considerable degree of material comfort.

But Ben Davis believed in justice. He believed that the Constitution applied to his people—equally with all others. That is how it came about that he offered his services to the International Labor Defense and became Herndon's lawyer.

That trial did a lot to change the course of his life. Describing that trial Davis said together with his client he "suffered some of the worst kind of treatment against Negroes. The judge in the case referred to me as a 'n----' and a 'darky' all the way through the case and to my client . . . treated me in such a way that I could see before me the whole treatment of the Negro people in the South where I had lived all my life."

"The fact that I had been a little luckier than the average Negro and in some ways, the average white, to have gotten such an education, was not at all effective in shielding me from what the Negroes had to suffer whether they were laborers or whether they were doctors or lawyers or men of wealth. . . . I considered what I could do at that moment that would enable me to hit the thing, this lynch system, this Jim Crow system. I considered that the best thing I could do was to join the Communist Party because that would hurt most, and so I did."

Ben had plenty of "hurt." As an associate of the International Labor Defense, headed by William L. Patterson, he participated in the now famous legal and mass defense of the framed nine Scottsboro Negro youths. He entered the defense of the Atlanta Six, Negro and white, who faced a conspiracy charge similar to Herndon. He helped edit the *Southern Worker*, which also meant in this land of "free speech" trying to find printers to print the paper.

In 1935 Ben became editor of the weekly *Negro Liberator* in New York City, then wrote for the *Daily Worker* and moved up to its editorial board. He ran for Congressman-at-large in 1942 and got 50,000 votes. In 1943 he was elected to the New York City Council with over 40,000 votes. In 1945, he was elected again to the Council—with more votes from white people than voted for [Christopher] Rankin in Mississippi—with 63,000 votes. His program was simple in words: "Make New York City a city without discrimination and injustice."

Of his program in the City Council, Ben told the Court: "I was there to represent the working people of New York City and I could do that by doing everything to stop the plunder of the big financiers and to stop their use of the City Council for their own interests."

From this clear statement of beliefs, the Court thought it had found something partisan. After all, it asked, wasn't Davis there to represent everybody? Ben replied dryly that since the monopolies were few and the working people and consumers pretty nearly represented everybody, he was satisfied with representing "pretty nearly everybody."

Ben Davis is a man who chose to risk many things and now finally his very freedom to represent and defend "pretty nearly everybody" against the privileged very few. There has not been a single case of injustice that Ben Davis has not raised his voice and pen against.

Whether it has been the defense of the honor and dignity of Negro womanhood, against legal lynching, or whether it has been his fight against the deathly rat-traps and tinder boxes in which some of our people live; whether against police brutality and terror which rides on well-groomed horses in the Harlem ghetto; or against the monopoly owners of our homes, our jobs and the very plots which claim our bodies in death which are Jim Crowed, Ben Davis' fearless and uncompromising voice has assailed the people's enemies.

An example of successful adoption of measures he proposed when a city council legislator, was the measure urging the New York City Congressional delegation to support enactment of pending Fair Employment legislation, for anti-lynch and anti-poll tax legislation.

Today with the job gains of Negro Americans, formerly strengthened by federal fair employment safeguards, almost a memory, can one truly imagine what Ben Davis' voice would mean demanding FEPC passage as against the shameful failure of the 83rd Congress to uphold a single election promise to enact any civil rights legislation?

Other measures Davis fought for and in some cases secured adoption were such varied measures as: granting the demands of merchant seamen for an increase of their basic wage rate; opposition to anti-labor legislation in Congress, jobs for all at trade union wages without discrimination; full job equality for Negro women; equal pay for equal work for women workers; increase in the New York City teacher salaries; greater monetary appropriations for our schools, increased state aid to New York City for education; appointment of a Negro to the New York City School Board; measures to protect the safety and lives of our kids in the antiquated structures called schools in the working class, Negro, Puerto Rican, Italian and Jewish communities.

Also, for restoration of the five cent fare on all subway and bus lines; demands for bans on biased textbooks and the lifting of bans on such books as authored by Mark Twain, Robert Louis Stevenson, Howard Fast and other outstanding writers; whose writings are feared. Davis urged restoration of progressive teachers to their posts and the exclusion of biased white supremacist and anti-Semitic instructors in our schools; cancellation of tax exemption to housing and redeveloping companies which practice discrimination against persons because of creed, race, color and national origin.

The magnificent fight finally achieved to break Jim Crow in Stuyvesant Town [a large private residential development on Manhattan's East Side) was led by Ben Davis during his four-year tenure in the City Council of New York for which he earned the enmity of the real estate lobby and Metropolitan Life Insurance Company. If today, New Yorkers celebrate Negro History Week, it is due to the consistent and the unflagging role of the Communist Party to set the record straight as to the heroic history of our people and to Davis' unanimously adopted measure in January 1944, to have New York's mayors proclaim this anniversary.

And if, when the baseball diamond, catching the shadow of the season's first ball, shiningly rings with the fan's plaudits for Negro athletes, a modest part of that struggle can be credited to Ben Davis and his Party.

If today the birthday of that scientific genius of Tuskegee, George Washington Carver, is officially proclaimed in New York by the mayor, it also is the result of a resolution introduced by Ben.

Ben Davis also fought the antecedents of the vicious McCarran and Walter–McCarran anti-foreign born legislation restricting West Indian immigration. He condemned such measures as a product of the whole reactionary campaign of hysteria against all of the foreign born, Negro and white, as well as against the Negro people, at the expense of West Indians first, the great majority of whom are staunch and militant fighters in this country (as well as in the Caribbean from whence their rich history springs) for Negro rights and full democracy.

And above and through it all was Ben's consistent record for international friendship and peace between nations based on negotiation of differences for national independence and freedom of all national and colonial oppressed peoples, for trade and cultural exchange between East and West.

Together with the late Hon. Peter V. Cacchione, first elected Communist legislator, Ben Davis' role as a fighting leader and people's legislator can be no more honorably termed—tribunes of the people!

But even this inadequate record does not give a full insight into Ben Davis, man, people's leader and proud Communist.

To get that one must seek out the people—they who know him, who have felt his hand, know his wisdom and have heard his great voice raised against oppression. We must seek out the people and listen to their voices.

They are legion who while not agreeing in toto with Ben Davis or the Communist Party, do agree that Ben Davis is a man of principle. They do agree that this man's fearless devotion to principle is to be respected. They do agree that one more day in jail is too long for Ben Davis who should never have been jailed for his ideas.

Two years ago, 13,000 people from Ben Davis's former district in Harlem, signed petitions demanding presidential amnesty for Davis and his colleagues. Now, if a man is to be judged, as the old saying goes, "by the company he keeps," he can best be estimated by the opinions of his contemporaries. From the day of Ben Davis' jailing and since that time, angry voices have been lifted among our people and our leaders as well as among white allies, to loose him and let him go!

Listen to their Voices:

"Ben Davis is a burning and shining light in these days of Cadillac leadership; he takes his place with the saints of old who went to jail for their opinions."

Reverend Dr. J. Pius Barbour

"Nobody considering Ben Davis as a man and a leader could by any stretch of the imagination think of him as guilty of anything but what this nation ought to reward and give the broadest chance for development. They need not necessarily follow him in all his opinions, but they must applaud the man, who, having the chance to be idle and careless, becomes busy, thoughtful and devoted and gives his life to the great cause of changing the methods of production and distribution of wealth in this country and in the world."

Dr. W. E. Burghardt Du Bois

"I stand firmly at the side of the convicted Communist Eleven. What happens to them is a deep concern of every American. . . . Shall we defend our true heritage or shall we allow ourselves to be destroyed by American fascism parading as defenders of the democratic faith?"

"Our powerful answer must be that Ben Davis may continue his fine contribution. Together with that answer must be provision and demand for arrest of judgment based on the true traditions of American justice."

"I am proud to say these few words for my dear friend and associate—Ben Davis."

Paul Robeson

"There is this . . . that must be admired about Du Bois, Robeson, Ben Davis and others. They are not taking it lying down. Ben Davis is in prison. . . . Robeson has sacrificed. . . . Du Bois has fought without let up for over half a century and at 85 he is determined as ever. Some day when truth gets a hearing, America, regardless of colour, we will honour them."

J. A. Rogers, Negro Historian

"It is time for non-Communists to drop their prejudices and do something and do it quickly or we will all be bound hand, foot and body."

"Negroes in the South are overthrowing the government of white supremacy every hour and we intend to continue doing it. There was a law saying Negroes couldn't vote. And we have been overthrowing that kind of government. When the government starts putting people in jail because it doesn't like their ideas then the liberties of 15 million Negroes are at stake."

"Harry T. Moore was sent to his death by a bomb and Benjamin J. Davis was sent to prison for the same reason. We cannot recall Harry T. Moore. But the American people can recall Ben Davis."

Mrs. Modjeska Simkins, Editor,
South Carolina Lighthouse and Informer

Numerous other prominent individuals have spoken out against the Smith Act. Among these are: Hon. Judge Hubert L. Delaney, Roscoe Dunjee, Editor of the Oklahoma *Black Dispatch,* Bishop William J. Walls, Dr. J. Pius Barbour, Editor, *National Baptist Voice,* Bishop C. C. Alleyne and others. Such widely differing political forces such as the CIO, AFL, independent unions, Americans for

Democratic Action, NAACP, churchmen, cultural leaders, educators and other prominent figures here and abroad, while themselves non-Communists and even anti-Communists, are alarmed over the threat to free speech by the jailing of Communists under the Smith Act. And two eminent Negro lawyers, Richard Westbrooks and Earl Dickerson of Chicago, in an historic *amicus curiae* brief urged reconsideration of the US Supreme Court 6–2 conviction of Ben Davis and his colleagues.

Ben Davis is not the only Negro leader who has been attacked by reaction as we can plainly see. But Ben Davis, Henry Winston, National Organizational Secretary of the Communist Party and the other Negro Communists under attack, were illegally seized, persecuted and harassed by reaction because they represent the most advanced sector of Negro leadership who link the Negro freedom fight to that of the working class and to the fight against war and fascism.

Reaction so fears the impact of Negro Communist leadership on the struggle for Negro freedom in our country, that an integral part of their anti-Negro offensive is the drive to jail and remove from leadership *all* leading Negro Communists in our country.

Today, Henry Winston, born in Hattiesburg, Mississippi, is a political refugee from the persecution of his country's government— a political refugee because he dared to expose and challenge the Jim Crow system of men like John Rankin from his hometown—a political refugee, because he dared along with his colleagues to expose and challenge the Korean War and because he proposed a system of society which would eliminate economic crises.

James E. Jackson, Jr., leading Negro Communist of Virginia, is similarly a political refugee. In a splendid pamphlet, written last year by his wife, Mrs. Esther Cooper Jackson, entitled *This Is My Husband,* Mrs. Jackson, mother of two children, wrote:

> "They accuse my husband of taking his 'dangerous ideas' out of books of 'foreigners' like Stalin and Lenin. . . .
> ". . . No, it is not dictation from any foreign source which caused my husband to dedicate his life and talents to the struggle for a new social order. Rather in the course of the struggle for a better life he discovered the answer to the

problems of our times which have grown as an integral part of the history of our country. That these ideas have been adopted in other lands simply indicates that mankind, facing common problem, eventually arrives at common answers."

For dedication of their lives to realizing the answers to the common problems of mankind over 115 Communist and working class leaders, 13 of whom are Negroes, have been arrested under the Smith Act.

These include, besides Ben Davis and Henry Winston, Pettis Perry of California and New York, Claudia Jones of New York, James Jackson, Jr. of Virginia, Thomas Dennis, Michigan, Ben Carreathers, Pittsburg, Pa., Al Murphy of Missouri and Alabama, Thomas Nabried, Philadelphia, Pa., Robert Campbell of New York and Ohio, Paul Bowen of Seattle, Washington, James Tate of Connecticut and Claude Lightfoot of Illinois.

The ruling class of our country well understands the historical significance of the rise of Negro Communist leadership in the United States. It is a leadership whose ideas and perspectives are based upon the scientific principles of Socialism, upon the conviction that full economic, political and social equality for the Negro people can only be won fully allied to the cause of the working class.

This new leadership arose in the [19]20s, grew rapidly in the [19]30s and strengthened its ties with the Negro community. Even today, held deep in the hearts of thousands of non-Communist Negro people, are memories of the struggles waged by the Communists against hunger, homelessness, joblessness and the misery of the Hoover depression.

What is more, the numerous and brilliant contributions made to the cause of Negro freedom—in the economic, political, social and cultural fields, by Negro and white Marxists have been recognized in all parts of the country by the Negro people.

Today, the very meaning of any serious leadership in the fight for Negro rights brings one into opposition with the foreign and domestic policies of government.

Ask yourself: Can anyone support the great national liberation struggles of the peoples of Africa—without facing the accusation of being a "*Communist*"?

Can anyone fight for the right to live in homes of our own choice—as in the Trumbull Homes in Illinois—without facing mob violence and the accusation of being a "*Communist*"? Can one invoke the First or Fifth Amendment, without the accusation of being a "*Communist*" who "*hides*" behind the "*protection*" (!) of the Constitution?

Whether in writings, speeches, or needed organization endeavors, *any* Negro leader who pursues *any necessary manifestation of leadership* is labeled "subversive," "communistic," "undesirable," "aliens," or "dangerous troublemakers."

Thus it is clear that while Negro leaders active in the Communist Party are singled out for special prosecution, the attacks extend far beyond the Communists. But in the struggle for full citizenship rights many different forces must unite for victory. . . .

Ben Davis Gets a "Hearing"

A FEDERAL JUDGE, member of the Federal Parole Board, described Ben Davis as the "most intelligent" prisoner he had ever interviewed and that he had found him a "sincere and fundamentally honest man."

A white Southerner by birth, the judge also told Ben Davis that any parole action in his case would be held up pending a full Board hearing in Washington, D.C.

Accordingly, a delegation headed by Paul Robeson, outstanding artist and life-long friend of Ben Davis; John Abt, Davis' present attorney; Mrs. Dolly Mason, community leader; Cyril Phillips, New York businessman; Rev. Kenneth Ripley Forbes of Philadelphia and Dr. Marcus Goldman, former Government geologist, appeared at a Federal Parole Board hearing February 11, 1953.

Their pleas were that Davis had served more than one-third of his sentence in the federal prison of Terre Haute and was now eligible for parole. Among other things raised by Robeson in a press conference was the tremendous sentiment for Davis' release in the Negro communities. Rev. Forbes said he communicated to the Board a feeling in the Negro communities throughout the nation for Davis' release.

Robeson further pointed out that in the recent Smith Act case involving the 13 Communist leaders, Judge Edward J. Dimmock had set the top sentence at three years, stating that Congress did not intend to apply the five-year sentence to conviction for "conspiracy to advocate."

Despite their pleas, the Parole Board, while listening politely, in a later decision, turned thumbs down on Davis' release.

Still another delegation went in February of this year to Brownell's office. The delegation in this case was headed by William L. Patterson, National Executive Secretary of the Civil Rights Congress, who was forced to serve a vindictive three-month sentence for not being able to produce *lost* names of his contributors to the Treasury Department; James W. Ford, National Executive Secretary, National Committee to Defend Negro Leadership; and Miss Louise Jeffers, Executive Secretary of the Harlem Committee to Free Ben Davis. This delegation presented petitions urging Davis' freedom and also left a memoranda [*sic*] with Senator Langer, Chairman of the Senate Judiciary Committee, which outlined the discriminatory practices suffered by Davis and other Negro prisoners in Terre Haute federal prison and demanded action by this Senate Committee.

Despite numerous petition campaigns, which have found a receptive echo and numerous anxious inquiries as to why Ben Davis is still in prison—HE *IS STILL NOT FREE!*

> ***With every ounce of strength***
> ***I shall continue to fight for the people.***
> —BENJAMIN J. DAVIS

In these words, Ben Davis opened his farewell speech to the people of his community and all his former constituents the night he spoke for the last time before his jailing in Harlem's famed Dewey Square.

The square was jammed with people and placards urging "Repeal the Smith Act!" "Free the Eleven Communist Leaders." "Stop Thought Control" and home-made signs scrawled "Ben, We Love You."

Some people had clenched fists, and tears of anger were in their eyes.

But Ben Davis continued to speak:

"The sun of liberty is rising all over the world . . ." He talked of
the unbreakable fraternity which we have with the peoples of Africa,
Asia, the West Indies, Europe, Latin and South America, who are
achieving national independence and freedom, as well as with the
peoples of the Soviet Union whose nation has wiped out racial discrimination and made it a crime. Ben spoke of our bonds with the
people in the wide world who fight for peace, equality, national
independence and security against atomic wars and for friendship
between nations.

And Ben said: "I'll be back on these Harlem streets some day;
I know I will. . . ." . . .

On the streets of Harlem one finds many people who know and
remember Ben Davis for his fight for the people's needs.

Here is a woman who remembers, how, when evicted, it was
Ben Davis and his Party, the Communist Party, who were among
the first to fight against her eviction, helped put her furniture back
in her house. Here is a bartender who asks, as you open a paper,
the *Daily Worker*, of which Ben Davis was publisher before he was
jailed, "How is Ben?"

Here is a Negro woman, whose sad eyes contrast strangely with
the strong lines in her stern face. I recognize her as the mother of
one of the five bereaved families from whom death claimed five
victims, three of whom were children and who lived in a firetrap in
Harlem. That was in January, 1947, when there were 45 deaths in
one month from slum housing in the Harlem-Puerto Rican Washington Heights area. "How is Mr. Davis?" She presses your hand
meaningfully.

Here is a Negro minister who, when you talk to him, quotes the
Scripture: "Smite Down the Shepherd and the Sheep Will Be Scat-
tered!" to show his understanding of Ben's jailing.

Here is a white couple who knew Ben and who ask: "What can
we do to help free Ben Davis?"

Two youths, Negro and white, striding arm in arm—they seem
like students—come up and say in the bright tones of youth: "We
Must Free Ben Davis!"

Yes, we can hear his voice! Even from behind prison bars, Davis'
fearless voice scathes racist Jim Crow!

And because it is the supreme evidence and continuation of his entire life's fight for his people, for all the oppressed, it is all the more resounding.

It is resounding, because it is *one* with the Negro leaders of the South who rallied in 15 states against the McCarthy tactics of the Jenner Committee, condemning them as a blow against the entire Negro community of the nation.

It is *one* with all those who fought to save Ethel and Julius Rosenberg and who fight to free Morton Sobell from a living death sentence of 30 years. It is *one* with the millions here and abroad who kept Wesley Wells from execution in the California gas chamber and who fight to free Mrs. Rosa Lee Ingram.

It is *one* with all our people who fight in these coming elections for an anti-McCarthy, pro-labour, pro-democratic Congress, for extended Negro representation, for peace, security and democracy!

It is *one* with all our people and our allies who fought and *won* reversal of the "separate but equal" doctrine of Southern schools' Jim Crow. And who fight to realize implementation *now* of the Supreme Court's ruling.

It is *one* with our brothers and sisters in the South, in Atlantic itself, in Ben's birthplace, in Dawson, Ga., who asked: "What are you doing to get Ben Davis out of prison?"

Ben Davis' voice and his fight for freedom is *one* with Jomo Kenyatta of Africa; Cheddi Jagan and Burnham of British Guiana; with Gabriel D'Arboussier of French Equatorial Africa; with all the valiant men and women fighters of all creeds and nations who fight for liberation and national independence in all parts of the world.

They've jailed Ben Davis. But his ideas are still abroad. It is Ben Davis himself who can best express his ideas from ladders on the streets of Harlem, in the broad arena of political and legislative struggle, in unity meetings with his people, Negro and white and with white allies, and in the councils of his own Party. Until Ben Davis can do so, the McCarthyites and the racists will have a strong weapon with which to spread fear and subversion.

Will you answer Ben's confidence that he will be back on the streets of Harlem—and all the broad highways of the nations of the day—soon?

The one answer—the one response to Davis' fight against prison Jim Crow and his jailing for his ideas is contained in the word—*AMNESTY!*

The fight to free men and women jailed for unpopular political beliefs by presidential amnesty is a great American tradition. There have been numerous cases of political amnesty in our country. Andrew Johnson's Republican Administration granted amnesty to conscientious objectors of World War I. President [Warren] Harding freed Eugene Debs, famed Socialist leader and other political prisoners as a result of a mass campaign which forced their freedom. And similar amnesty decrees were issued by President Calvin Coolidge.

Surely—there is need for unity of all democratic-loving Americans to free Ben Davis—to demand amnesty for all political prisoners. Especially is this true of the Negro people as a whole, who first understand that the jailing of Ben Davis, *in the prime of his life*, is the jailing of a part of our historic struggle for full citizenship rights in these United States!

Epilogue

In post–World War II America, the internal turmoil brought on by the Cold War, the Smith Act prosecutions, and the ouster of Earl Browder as general secretary led to an internal battle in which the Communist Party expelled a number of members who were accused of displaying "white chauvinism." In 1949 and 1950, the CPUSA was driven out of the industrial unions of the Congress of Industrial Organizations (CIO) and much of the American labor movement. A significant number of leaders of the CPUSA viewed their organizational efforts among the white working class as unsuccessful. Instead, they would now focus on mobilizing and leading the black working class as the "vanguard of the revolution."

Black Communists saw their party endure during the 1950s and 1960s through the defections after Nikita Khrushchev's speech in 1956 attacking Stalin's "crimes" and subsequent sectarian splits. Indeed, the CPUSA made efforts to reestablish itself among university students and American youth in general through W.E.B. Du Bois Clubs. Du Bois, of course, strides through American history as an icon. He was a great social scientist, author of such classics as the Souls of Black Folk *and* Black Reconstruction, *and an original founder the NAACP. In the following document, Du Bois tells in a letter why at ninety he wished to become a "card-carrying Communist." Soon afterward, he moved to*

Ghana (the first of the black African colonies gain freedom from white European colonial domination). He settled there and died two years later. He had joined the CPUSA in 1961.

▪ ▪ ▪

To Gus Hall,
Communist Party of the USA
New York, New York

On this first day of October 1961, I am applying for admission to membership in the Communist Party of the United States. I have been long and slow in coming to this conclusion, but at last my mind is settled.

In college I heard the name of Karl Marx, but read none of his works, nor heard them explained. At the University of Berlin, I heard much of those thinkers who had definitively answered the theories of Marx, but again we did not study what Marx himself had said. Nevertheless, I attended meetings of the Socialist Party and considered myself a Socialist.

On my return to America, I taught and studied for sixteen years. I explored the theory of Socialism and studied the organized social life of American Negroes; but still I neither read nor heard much of Marxism. Then I came to New York as an official of the new NAACP and editor of the *Crisis Magazine*. The NAACP was capitalist orientated and expected support from rich philanthropists.

But it had a strong Socialist element in its leadership in persons like Mary Ovington, William English Walling and Charles Edward Russell. Following their advice, I joined the Socialist Party in 1911. I knew then nothing of practical Socialist politics and in the campaign of 1912, I found myself unwilling to vote the Socialist Party rules and consequently I resigned from the Socialist Party.

For the next twenty years I tried to develop a political way of life for myself and my people. I attacked the Democrats and Republicans for monopoly and disfranchisement of Negroes; I attacked the Socialists for trying to segregate Southern Negro members; I praised the racial attitudes of the Communists, but opposed their tactics in the case of the Scottsboro boys and their advocacy of a Negro state. At the same time I began to study Karl Marx and the

Communists; I read *Das Kapital* and other communist literature; I hailed the Russian Revolution of 1917, but was puzzled at the contradictory news from Russia.

Finally in 1926, I began a new effort: I visited Communist lands. I went to the Soviet Union in 1926, 1936, 1949, and 1959; I saw the nation develop. I visited East Germany, Czechoslovakia and Poland. I spent ten weeks in China, traveling all over the land. Then, this summer, I rested a month in Rumania.

I was early convinced that Socialism was an excellent way of life, but I thought it might be reached by various methods. For Russia I was convinced she had chosen the only way open to her at the time. I saw Scandinavia choosing a different method, half-way between Socialism and Capitalism. In the United States I saw Consumers Cooperation as a path from Capitalism to Socialism, while England, France and Germany developed in the same direction in their own way. After the depression and the Second World War, I was disillusioned. The progressive movement in the United States failed. The Cold War started. Capitalism called Communism a crime.

Capitalism cannot reform itself; it is doomed to self-destruction. No universal selfishness can bring social good to all.

Communism—the effort to give all men what they need and to ask of each the best they can contribute—that is the only way of human life. It is a difficult and hard end to reach—it has and will make mistakes, but today it marches triumphantly on in education and science, in home and food with increased freedom of thought and deliverance from dogma. In the end Communism will triumph. I want to help bring that day.

The path of the American Communist Party is clear: It will provide the United Sates with a real Third Party and thus restore democracy to this land. It will call for:

1. Public ownership of natural resources and of all capital.
2. Public control of transportation and communications.
3. Abolition of poverty and limitation of personal income.
4. No exploitation of labor.
5. Social medicine, with hospitalization and care of the old.

6. Free education for all.
7. Training for jobs and jobs for all.
8. Discipline for growth and reform.
9. Freedom under law.
10. No dogmatic religion.

These aims are not crimes. They are practiced all over the world. No nation can call itself free which does not allow its citizens to work for these ends.

Selected Bibliography

Anderson, Carol. "Bleached Souls and Red Negros: The NAACP and Black Communists in the early Cold War, 1948–1952." In *The Achievement of American Liberalism: The New Deal and Its Legacies*, ed. William Henry Chafe. New York: Columbia University Press, 2003.

Allen, James S. *Negro Liberation*. New York: International Publishers, 1938.

Baldwin, Kate A. *Beyond the Color Line and the Iron Curtain: Reading Encounters between Black and Red, 1922–1963*. Durham, NC: Duke University Press, 2002.

Berland, Oscar. "The Communist Perspective on the 'Negro Question' in America, 1919–1931." *Science and Society* 63–64, nos. 2 and 4 (Winter–Summer 1999–2000).

———. "Nasanov and the Comintern's American Negro Program." *Science and Society* 65, no. 2 (2001).

Blakely, Allison. *Russia and the Negro: Blacks in Russian History and Thought*. Washington, DC: Howard University Press, 1986.

Bornet, Vaughn D. "Historical Scholarship, Communism, and the Negro." *Journal of Negro History* 37, no. 3 (July 1952).

Campbell, Susan. "'Black Bolsheviks' and Recognition of African-American's Right to Self-Determination by the Communist Party U.S.A." *Science and Society* 58, no. 4 (1994–1995).

Carter, Dan T. *Scottsboro: A Tragedy of the American South*. Baton Rouge: Louisiana State University Press, 1979.

Davies, Carole Boyce. *Left of Karl Marx: The Political Life of Black Communist Claudia Jones*. Durham, NC: Duke University Press, 2007.

Davis, Benjamin J. *Communist Councilman from Harlem: Autobiographical Notes Written in a Federal Penitentiary.* New York: International Publishers, 1969.

Edwards, Brent Hayes. "Dossier on Black Radicalism: Introduction: The Autonomy of Black Radicalism." *Social Text* 19, no.2 (2001).

Enckefort, Maria. "The Life and Work of Otto Huiswoud: Professional Revolutionary and Internationalist (1893–1961)." Ph.D. diss., University of the West Indies, 2008.

Eversole, Theodore W. "Benjamin J. Davis, Jr. (1903–1964): From Republican Atlanta Lawyer to Harlem Communist Councilman." *Journal of the Afro-American Historical and Genealogical Society* 8, no. 1 (1987).

Foner, Philip Sheldon. *American Socialism and Black Americans from the Age of Jackson to World War II.* Westport, CT: Greenwood Press, 1977.

Foner, Philip Sheldon, and James S. Allen, eds. *American Communism and Black Americans: A Documentary History, 1919–1929.* Philadelphia: Temple University Press, 1987.

Foner, Philip Sheldon, and Herbert Shapiro, eds. *American Communism and Black Americans: A Documentary History, 1930–1934.* Philadelphia: Temple University Press, 1991.

Ford, James W. *The Negro and the Democratic Front.* New York: International Publishers, 1938.

Gardner, John L. "African Americans in the Soviet Union in the 1920s and 1930s: The Development of Transcontinental Protest." *Western Journal of Black Studies* 23, no. 3 (1999).

Goldfield, Michael. "The Decline of the Communist Party and the Black Question in the U.S.: Harry Haywood's Black Bolshevik." *Review of Radical Political Economics* 12, no. 1 (1980).

Goodman, James E. *Stories of Scottsboro.* New York: Pantheon Books, 1994.

Gore, Dayo F. *Radicalism at the Crossroads: African American Women Activists in the Cold War.* New York: New York University Press, 2011.

Gore, Dayo F., Jeanne Theoharis, and Komozi Woodard, eds. *Want to Start a Revolution?: Radical Women in the Black Freedom Struggle.* New York: New York University Press, 2009.

Grigsby, Daryl Russell. *For the People: Black Socialists in the United States, Africa, and the Caribbean.* San Diego: Asante Publications, 1987.

Harris, Leshawn. "Running with the Reds: African American Women and the Communist Party during the Great Depression." *Journal of African American History* 94, no. 1 (January 2009).

Haywood, Harry. *The Road to Negro Liberation: The Tasks of the Communist Party in Winning Working Class Leadership of the Negro Liberation Struggles, and the Fight against Reactionary Nationalist-Reformist Movements among the Negro People.* New York: Workers Library, 1934.

———. *Black Bolshevik: Autobiography of an Afro-American Communist.* Chicago: Liberator Press, 1978.

Hill, Robert A. "Racial and Radical: Cyril V. Briggs, the *Crusader* Magazine, and the African Blood Brotherhood, 1918–1922." In *The Crusader,* ed. Cyril V. Briggs. New York: Garland, 1987.

Hooker, James R. *Black Revolutionary: George Padmore's Path from Communism to Pan-Africanism.* New York: Praeger, 1967.

Horne, Gerald. *Studies in Black: Progressive Views and Reviews of the African-American Experience.* Dubuque, IA: Kendall/Hunt, 1992.

———. *Black Liberation/Red Scare: Ben Davis and the Communist Party.* Newark: University of Delaware Press, 1993.

———. "The Red and the Black: The Communist Party and African-Americans in Historical Perspective." In *New Studies in the Politics and Culture of U.S. Communism,* ed. Michael E. Brown, Randy Martin, Frank Rosengarten, and George Snedeker. New York: Monthly Review Press, 1993.

Howard, Walter T. *B. D. Amis, African American Radical: A Short Anthology of Writings and Speeches.* Lanham, MD: University Press of America, 2007.

———. *Black Communists Speak on Scottsboro: A Documentary History.* Philadelphia: Temple University Press, 2008.

Hutchinson, Earl Ofari. *Blacks and Reds: Race and Class in Conflict, 1919–1990.* East Lansing: Michigan State University Press, 1995.

Jackson, James E. *Revolutionary Tracings.* New York: International Publishers, 1974.

James, Winston. *Holding Aloft the Banner of Ethiopia: Caribbean Radicalism in Early Twentieth-Century American.* London: Verso, 1998.

Jennings, La Vinia. "Louise Thompson." In *Notable Black American Women,* ed. Jessie Carney Smith. Detroit: Gale Research, 1992.

Johanningsmeier, Edward. "Communists and Black Freedom Movements in South Africa and the U.S.: 1919–1950." *Journal of Southern African Studies* 30, no. 1 (March 2004).

Kanet, Roger. "The Comintern and the 'Negro Question': Communist Policy in the United States and Africa, 1921–1941." *Survey* 19, no. 4 (Autumn 1973).

Kelley, Robin D. G. *Hammer and Hoe: Alabama Communists during the Great Depression.* Chapel Hill: University of North Carolina Press, 1984.

———. "Patterson, Louise Thompson." In *Black Women in America,* vol. 2, ed. Darlene Clark Hine. Brooklyn, NY: Carlson, 1993.

———. *Race Rebels: Culture, Politics, and the Black Working Class.* New York: Free Press and Maxwell Macmillan, 1994.

————. "But a Local Phase of World Problem: Black History's Global Vision, 1883–1950." *Journal of American History* 86, no. 3 (December 1999).

Kellner, Bruce. "Thompson [Patterson], Louise." In *The Harlem Renaissance: A Historical Dictionary for the Era.* Westport, CT: Greenwood Press, 1984.

Klehr, Harvey, and William Tompson. "Self-Determination in the Black Belt: Origins of a Communist Policy." *Labor History* 30, no 3. (Summer 1989).

Klore, Joe. "Harlem's Communist Councilman, Ben Davis Jr." *Political Affairs* 81, no. 2 (2002).

Kornweibel, Theodore, Jr. *"Seeing Red": The Federal Campaign against Black Militancy,* 1919–1925. Bloomington: Indiana University Press, 1998.

Kosa, John, and Clyde.Z. Nunn. "Race, Deprivation and Attitude toward Communism." *Phylon* 25, no. 4 (1964).

Marable, Manning. "Why Black Americans Are Not Socialists." In *Socialist Perspectives,* ed. Phyllis Jacobson and Julius Jacobson. Princeton, NJ: Karz-Cohl, 1983.

Markowitz, Norman."Benjamin Davis, Jr.: Centennial, 1903–2003." *Political Affairs* 82, no. 2 (February 2003).

Martin, Charles H. "The International Labor Defense and Black Americans." *Labor History* 26, no. 2 (Spring 1985).

McClellan, Woodford. "Africans and Black Americans in the Comintern Schools, 1925–1934." *International Journal of African Historical Studies* 26, no. 2 (1993).

McDuffie, Erik. *Sojourning for Freedom: Black Women, American Communism, and the Making of Black Left Feminism.* Durham, NC: Duke University Press, 2011.

Miller, James A., Susan D. Pennybacker, and Eve Rosenhaft. "Mother Ada Wright and the International Campaign to Free the Scottsboro Boys." *American Historical Review* 106, no. 2 (April 2001).

Murray, Hugh T., Jr. "The NAACP versus the Communist Party: The Scottsboro Rape Cases, 1931–1932." *Phylon* 28, no. 3 (1967).

————. "Aspects of the Scottsboro Campaign." *Science and Society* 32, no. 2 (Summer 1971).

————. "Changing America and the Changing Image of Scottsboro." *Phylon* 38, no. 1 (1977).

Naison, Mark. "Marxism and Black Radicalism in America: Notes on a Long (and Continuing) Journey." *Radical America* 5, no. 3 (May–June 1971).

————. "Communism and Black Nationalism in the Depression: The Case of Harlem." *Journal of Ethnic Studies* 2, no. 2 (Summer 1974).

————. "The Communist Party in Harlem: 1928–1936." Ph.D. diss., Columbia University, New York, 1976.

————. "The Communist Party in Harlem in the Early Depression years: A Case Study in the Reinterpretation of American Communism." *Radical History Review*, no. 3 (Fall 1976).

————. "Harlem Communists and the Politics of Black Protest." *Marxist Perspectives* 1, no. 3 (Fall 1978).

————. "Historical Notes on Blacks and American Communism: The Harlem Experience." *Science and Society* 42, no. 3 (Fall 1978).

————. "*Communists in Harlem during the Depression.* Urbana: University of Illinois Press, 1983.

Nadasen, Pam. "Thompson, Louise." In *Encyclopedia of African-American Culture and History,* vol. 5, ed. Jack Salzman, David Lionel Smith, and Cornel West. New York: Macmillan Library Reference, 1996.

Nolan, William Anthony. *Communism versus the Negro.* Chicago: H. Regnery, 1951.

O'Reilly, Kenneth. *Racial Matters: The FBI's Secret File on Black America, 1960–1972.* New York: Free Press, 1991.

Parascandola, Louis J. "Cyril Briggs and the African Blood Brotherhood: A Radical Counterpoint to Progressivism." *New York Life and History* (January 2006).

Patterson, William L. *The Man Who Cried Genocide: An Autobiography.* New York: International Publishers, 1971.

Record, Wilson. *The Negro and Communist Party.* Chapel Hill: University of North Carolina Press, 1951.

————. "The Development of the Communist Position on the Negro Question in the United States." *Phylon* 19, no. 3 (Fall 1958).

————. *Race and Radicalism: The NAACP and the Communist Party in Conflict.* Ithaca, NY: Cornell University Press, 1964.

————. "American Radical Ideologies and Organizations in Transition." *Phylon* 26, no. 4 (1965).

Rywkin, Michael. "Black Americans: A Race of Nationality? Some Communist Viewpoints." *Canadian Review of Studies in Nationalism* 3, no. 1 (1975).

Solomon, Mark. "Red and Black: Negroes and Communism, 1929–1932." Ph.D. diss., Harvard University, Cambridge, MA, 1972.

————. Red and Black: *Communists and Afro-Americans, 1929–1935.* New York: Garland, 1988.

————. *The Cry Was Unity: Communists and African Americans, 1917–36.* Jackson: University Press of Mississippi, 1998.

Spark, Clare. "Race, Caste, or Class? The Bunche–Myrdal Dispute over an American Dilemma." *International Journal of Politics, Culture, and Society* 14, no. 3 (Spring 2001).

Sullivan, William C. "Communism and the American Negro." *Religion in Life* 37, no. 4 (1968).

Thomas, Theman. "Cyril Briggs and the African Blood Brotherhood: Another Radical View of Race and Class during the 1920s." Ph.D. diss., University of California, Santa Barbara, 1981.

Thomas, Tony. "Black Nationalism and Confused Marxists." *Black Scholar* 4, no. 1 (1972).

Turner, W. Burghardt, and Joyce Moore Turner, eds. *Richard B. Moore, Caribbean Militant in Harlem: Collected Writings, 1920–1972.* Bloomington: University of Indiana Press, 1989.

Van West, Carroll. "Perpetuation the Myth of America: Scottsboro and Its Interpreters." *South Atlantic Quarterly* 80 (1981).

Van Zanter, John W. "Communist Theory and the American Negro Question." *Review of Politics* 29, no. 4 (1967).

Wald, Alan. "The U.S. Left and Anti-Racism." In *Black Liberation and the American Dream: The Struggle for Racial and Economic Justice: Analysis, Strategy, Readings,* ed. Paul Le Blanc. Amherst, NY: Humanity Books, 2003.

———. "New Black Radical Scholarship." *Against the Current,* no. 108 (January–February 2004).

Wexley, John. "They Shall Not Die." In *Proletarian Literature in the United States: An Anthology,* ed. Granville Hicks and Joseph Freeman. New York: International Publishers, 1935.

Williams, Henry. *Black Response to the American Left: 1917–1929.* Princeton, NJ: Princeton University Press, 1973.

Williams, Lynn Barstis. "Images of Scottsboro." *Southern Cultures* 6, no. 1 (2000).

Wynn, Daniel Webster. *The NAACP versus Negro Revolutionary Protest: A Comparative Study of the Effectiveness of Each Movement.* New York: Exposition Press, 1955.

Index